# THE
# COSMIC
# CONNECTION

## A Special Collection of Poems from the 60's & 70's.

> "For words, like nature,
>
> Half reveal, and half conceal
>
> The soul within."
>
> *Alfred Lord Tennyson*
> In memoriam. A.H.H. 1850

By the late Fler Beaumont

Copyright © Andrea Beaumont, daughter / executor for the late Fler Beaumont 2021

First published by Busybird Publishing 2022

Copyright © 2022 Andrea Beaumont for the late Fler Beaumont.

**ISBN:**
978-1-922691-76-7

This work is copyright. Apart from any use permitted under the *Copyright Act 1968*, no part of this publication may be reproduced, stored in a retrieval system or transmitted in any form or by any means, electronic, mechanical, photocopying, recording or otherwise, without the prior written permission of Andrea Beaumont and Publisher.

**Cover Image:** - NASA, Star images - Pole Star Publications LTD U.K. 2006
**Cover design:** Busybird Publishing, A Beaumont
**Layout and typesetting**: Busybird Publishing

Busybird Publishing
2/118 Para Road
Montmorency, Victoria
Australia 3094
www.busybird.com.au

# The Dedication

This is the work of the late Fler Beaumont (passed to higher life 01/09/2019). She was a prolific poet and author (previous Poetry book 'The Eternal Door - A Special Collection of Divine Love Poems 2021').

This volume by Fler came through a walk-in. This entity was known as Peter Mardon. His spirit wrote these poems, during the 1960s & 1970s.

It is an honour to reproduce this work, titled "The Cosmic Connection.
(A Special Collection of Poems from the 60's & 70's)."

"The mystic Seer stands with his seven black doves. His words are of times past and present."*☆

*from a spiritual source.

Permission granted to Andrea Beaumont by Fler Beaumont during her lifetime for this material to be published posthumously.

Andrea Beaumont – daughter & executor.

# The Morning of Our Love

The morning of our love
woke quietly
as the bud opens
unfolding velvet fingers
to the sun's bright orb.

The first dew shone
like liquid stars
caught upon our parted lips.

We shared a kiss
encompassing
all of heaven and hell
and found ourselves
spread upon
the camisole of earth.

© Peter Mardon 1968.

# Being One

I complete your body
you complete mine

As morning ignites
we are fused

one body one soul
one spirit

each giving to the other
living in the other
loving
being one …

© P. Mardon 1968.

# Awake

Day is bursting at the seams
yet you are not here
beside me

O restive one
do you pause beside
a crystal fountain
searching its reaching arms
for suggestions?

or do you
stand beside a pine-tree
counting its needles
comparing their number to
the number of minutes
you spend away
from me?

Awake! Arise! I move
toward you in every
direction
yet each direction
takes me away from you

only if you move too
can we meet again.

© P. Mardon 1968.

# The Enshrined Flower

The pure, white flower grows within
The sheltered shrine, untouched by sin
Its petals are undefiled
And chaste, like Heaven's fairest child.
Though wild the wind that hovers near,
The sacred flower knows no fear.
Within the shrine the air is calm,
The Dweller cannot come to harm.
The alabaster shrine so pure,
Throughout the ages does endure.
This tender blossom, white and free,
Now rests within its sanctuary.
An unseen Spirit tends the bloom
And drinks the sweet and pure perfume.
An unseen eye watches with care
The lovely flower resting there.
Around the shrine the World does turn
As all mankind their lessons learn.
The Pure, white flower watches all,
as kingdoms rise and kingdoms fall,
The flower oft-times dreams a dream,
As drifting down sweet slumber's stream.
It seems that in the World's mad race,
The flower, also, measures pace.
But soon the sleeping Dreamer wakes,
As Ennell's dawning softly breaks.
'Twas but a dream, and flower white
Still does dwell within the Light.
The alabaster shrine enfolds
The pure, white flower; see how holds
The sacred shrine its precious trust
Within its arms. No drosser dust
Shall ever mar its petals fair
While dwells the pure, white flower there.

© P. M. 1968.

# Okum Frog

No bone there was for Canus Dog,
And solemn was the day,
But swiftly hopped the Okum Frog,
And said "The price I'll pay!"

The Miller ground exceeding fine,
Until the rock was dust,
But underground the Turtle's mine
Gave gold, as gold it must.

The grinding of the Mill increased
And soon was gone the gold,
But crying of the Bluebird ceased.
For story was he told.

A fairy-tale, a fairy-tale!
Here comes the Happy Prince!
Why then does my love grow pale,
And disappears long since?

The Tinsel Fairy waves his wand,
And says "Behold, I'm One!"
But swiftly hops from out the pond,
The Frog Prince who has None.

The apple tree has shed her tear.

© P. Mardon 1969.

# Morning at Eleven

Every morning at eleven I die
there's no glamour in my death
no firing of guns no trumpets blow

it is just as though nothing has happened
one moment I am there
the next moment I am gone

nobody takes any notice
because it happens so often
it is as regular as the morning coffee-break

I suppose if I did not die at eleven one morning
it would cause a mild disturbance
people don't like their clockwork world to change

it's almost elven now funny how desirable
life becomes when you are just about to lose it
the sky seems almost too blue for sky

more like sleeping fields of cornflowers
or a magic carpet made of forget-me-nots
"forget-me-not" yes, each time that I die

I pray that the world will forget me not
I pray that I shall return again as always
I pray that it will not be my final departure

as I feel myself going each morning at eleven
I remember the warmth of the sun
the fresh delight of the cool Spring breeze

I remember neat suburban houses
and rows of golden daffodils
a lake shining in the sun

children's laughter and swallows swooping
over moss-green lawns
but most of all I remember you

you with your sunshine smile
your cool-breeze touch
your forget-me-not eyes

and I want to live to come back
and I shall of course come back
I always do

at precisely five minutes past eleven
I always return
and life continues its ordered pattern

the boss is very kind and understanding
he never deducts the missing five minutes
from my pay-envelope

even though it happens every morning at eleven
as it is going to happen now
there go the pips

one two three four
five six seven eight
nine ten eleven

eleven! ... but I'm still here
something is wrong
I stir uneasily in my chair

my heart thumping like the doomsday drum
and my mouth as dry and hot as Hades' coals
trembling I turn and look about

they're all here filling their cups with coffee
lighting cigarettes then suddenly
they realise that I am still here

an uneasy hush falls over the whole office
faces are puzzled, strained, tense
something has gone wrong with the set pattern

deathly-still silence hangs like a shroud
then through the stillness
a girl begins to whimper

suspicion, fear and terror
take hold of my puzzled friends
something is rising through it all

like a screaming bird of prey
then it breaks panic seizes
one of the present unfortunates

and sends him shrieking to my side
eyes like fearful coals
burning at me through me

pleading with me not to be there
but I am there
it cannot be altered

with a strangled sob of futility
he grasps the paper-weight on my desk
and smashes smashes smashes

-3-

at my shouldn't-be-there head
until only the shattered clockwork remains
but still the carcasse abuses

a great moaning sets up
although he beats me to a pulp
until I as a person am no longer distinguishable

the pieces remain
the pulp, the broken bones, the blood
remain a mute testimony

that something is still wrong
they gather me up carrying the pieces
in the girls' silk scarves

and deposit the mess in the incinerator
downstairs shutting the door
they breathe a communal sigh of relief

wash their hands and scrub the floor
until no vestige remains to tell
that I had been there where I shouldn't have been

now everything is normal again
the office routine can continue
but this time I know

that I shall not return.

© Peter Mardon 1968.

# The Painter

I knew a man ;
his legs were an easel,
his hands were a palette
and his fingers were
multi-coloured paint-
brushes ; his
mind

      a kaleidoscope
of colours, rushing
one into another; spurting,
splashing, slipping, sliding
      blending there
forever ;

alizarin-crimson, wild
vermilion, umber and
sienna – burnt and
raw ;
      these were his
world ; his pattern
of life

      was etched upon
a canvas. Wise man, to
have perpetuated his
soul

© P. Mardon 1970.

# Shift.

I awoke from sleep to
find that I had been
transposed to another
place, another form.
Unfamiliar surroundings
Crept mutely in upon
me, whispering of change
but not explaining why.

Pale moonlight trembled
through the window
outlining stark iron
bars against a sullen
silent sky. Unfamiliar
hands wiped beads of
perspiration from my brow.

Where was I? Who
was I? The questions
chased each other through
a ragged brain. Where
had memory gone? Who
had drained it dry
and left not one
drop to aid my state?

There was no answer
to the riddle even
when they led me
out and put the rope
around my neck. Even
as I fell, and felt
the snap, I still
did not know …….

© P. Mardon 1970.

# A New Dawn

You left
I was alone
I wept
No longer was there world
No sight
No sound

A solitary sound rushed across the
silence of my heart
Some-one asked
"Who are you?"

My world began anew

© P. Mardon 1970.

# Little Girl Lost

They didn't know
The girl was
Not quite there;

neither would they
have cared,
if they had known.

"Get lost !"
they told her.

Three years later
we are
still
searching …..

© By Peter Mardon 1970.

# Mushroom

bridge storm coat so
threadbare
rickety over marshy
water
wind-leaves lash
skin already wet

debris

sticks decaying leaves
squelch under-foot
path of travel-one
clothes like starving
leech cling
male
piercing eyes penetrate

on on on

upward over boughs
fallen
spectre comes to meet
falls like
wet sheet to
ground
eating sodden brown

on on on

uphill to left
giant mushroom
eat
diminish
small smaller
⅛ th of an inch

mushroom door open
fanfare in hall of
remember
lost inheritance

"father!" cries, feet
run arms outstretch
home at last
journey there back here
complete

floor rocks
walls away
ceiling rumbles

fanfare disjointed
quake
panic
\*\*\*
little girl's hands
clutch
wants mother's smile

mushroom

"mummy, is this one
alright?"

"yes, darling"

mushroom uprooted
basket full

© By Peter Mardon 1970.

# The Ascent

it was the final three steps
that finished me
the other nine hundred
and ninety-seven

didn't mean a thing
they were a reason for existence
a means to an end
they didn't mean a thing

at first it was like a game
it was a game
seeing how any i could
cover at one leap

but it soon became a tedium
and i had to devise other means
to keep interest going
it wasn't too hard

i tried climbing up backward
but then i could only see
what i had left behind
not much interest in that

then i tried the sideward step
a little more interesting
to see what had been missed
lying there un-noticed at the side

depression soon put an end to that
what next?
Eyes closed of course

It was surprizing how quickly

i grew accustomed to the dark
after a few stumbling steps
almost losing balance
i became quite adept at the art

inward thoughts were suddenly freed
the world lost its perspective
grains of sand were magnified
and mountains disappeared

but curiosity won the toss
and i found that
had climbed so high
that i became dazedly dizzy

falling upon my knees
clutching frantically at
the stone grey steps beneath me
i prayed for strength to continue

almost choking on my fear
i crawled like a worm
up up up
until

but three steps remained
deathly fear and terror
of unknown things
took hold of me

what had i been moving toward ?
where was i headed ?
what would be my reward

-2-

when the goal was reached?

i could not bear to learn
the answer
i knew where i had come from
i did not know where i would go

with a mighty leap
i left those steps
and as i hurtled downward
i knew where i was going

© By Peter Mardon 1970.

# The End

Whither flows the river?
Whither falls the rain?
Who becomes the giver?
Where lies loss and gain?

Every man is friend and foe;
cobwebs make a crown;
duty wears the face of woe,
upward wanders down.

Turtles keep on walking.
Sol keeps shining bright.
silent voices talking,
eyes that see at night.

Is there sand upon the beach?
Waves upon the sea?
Is it near, or out of reach?
Will it ever be?

Walrus weeps upon the shore;
Moon conceals his name;
carpenter calls out for more;
serpent enters game.

Black dove seeks a distant star,
hawks wear scarlet plumes,
fools are holding seminar,
flower hide their blooms.

Weary feet run to the race;
red and blue make blend;
judge and jury hide their face;
welcome to the end.

© By Peter Mardon 1970.

# Work Day

      like robots
set upon a given course
marching
      unerringly
towards their destination
not thinking
and
not caring
        drawn
magnetically
to the
open jaws
     awaiting
anticipating
perhaps, today,
       some
new taste,
some
fresh spark of life
     evolved
since
     yesterday's famine
gnashing today's offering

   the giant moans
     ever the same
no change
   like
   crawling corpses
   mingled
   like patterns from
   a mould
belching,
   the bloated giant
  spews them forth
onto the gaping streets
     where
   like maggots
they crawl
   home
  to await again
their
   morning call

© By Peter Mardon 1970.

# Domino

        drawing the veil across  
time-weary eyes  
                i retreat  
into  
        the quiet sanctuary  
of  
        my secluded mind  
         *

        Cybele drapes  
                motionless  
across her throne,  
                    one marbled  
                    hand  
            shading eyes  
too full of secrets  
                 the other  
    caressing a  
          silent sphinx  
        *

    the vault is  
        shadowed-grey; all  
            has ceased  
gone  
        the illusion of life  
    forgotten  
               my  
                      pseudo-friends

reality
       surrounds
                my soul
            and thoughts
are freed
        of rusted shackles
      too long
            worn

    *

  like the dawning of
time's
      first awakening,
      Cybele's smile
     begins,
        inscrutable ;
reflecting
      lapis-lazuli-eyes
   fluorescent
       in this
shadowed crypt
    of
      unknown thoughts
and veiled reality

    *

  sudden flash of coralline
illumines
      spectral-grey ;
        damasks my

-2-

             sequestered screen ;
                                         eclipse
                    deserts a
                              saffron-sun
             harlequin
                         appears
                                   flinging
             streaks of
                          amber, heliotrope
                    and
                          crimson
                                   across
             my silent
                          shroud
                              *
                mystery is
                          shattered and
             becomes a
                    thousand glittering
             stars
                in a peacock sky ;
                                   kaleidoscope
                  clatters against
                                my opal-
                                        brain
                              *

                amethystine angels
                                scatter lilacs
                          and roses burst in
                                        carmine
             from

                                                  -3-

        the sky

           *

    sphinx, no longer
                silent
starts
      to purr
          and like
a downy cat,
          stretches in
              the sun

         *

    Cybele begins
          to dance, and
      sings a
              crystal-song,
and I again
         respond
      to join
         the
parhelion
      parade

        *

© P. M. 1970.

-4-

# Peace

Today is a day of infinite rest
there is peace in our house
the children are silent and
even my mother-in-law is quiet
there is no dust on the furniture
the floors are polished
the beds are made and
the ironing is done
everyone is neat and clean.

Today is a day of infinite rest
there is peace in our house
a knock at the door
footsteps in the hall
polite voices
a cup of tea?      yes please
sugar?         two please
everything is in order

Today is a day of infinite rest
there is peace in our house
a car has arrived
mummy can I sit in the front seat?
no dear    why not?    hush dear
footsteps in the hall again
hands lifting
coffin moving
I
    am
        on
            my
                way
                ...

© By Peter Mardon 1970.

# There is a Prison

There is a prison
each man makes
rocks bars chains
the seams
the charred remains
of yesterday's dreams
rotted moulded
turned to dust.

He shakes
the tattered earth
scorched scalded
tries to start anew
he must
renew.

He finds
the dearth
too deep;
the chains of yesterday
made of bitter steel
too real;

He rushes on
to sleep
behind the blinds
of clay.

© By Peter Mardon 1970.

# Nomis

A strange, tattered figure – He sits on his throne;
If "throne" can be called and old bamboo chair
He dwells in a world that is his, all alone,
And watches the dancing circlets of air.

He wears a strange cloak, of rare, weird design
And his crown is a head-dress as wizards might wear.
He laughs at the Gods, and he mocks the divine,
And millions of worlds take light from his hair.

The Cavern of Nomis has seen the Parade;
The dark eyes of Nomis hold secrets untold;
Yes, let the full measure of everything fade,
and Nomis still sits there – The Wizard of Old.

© By Peter Mardon 1970.

# Autumn Song

        we were two  
  floating  
    autumn leaves  
      brown and gold  
        russet and tan  

leaping  
dancing  
      across countryside  
        all foreign to our  
          kind of joy  

chasing  
following  
      each other  
        sometimes  
mingling  
      quietly together  
        by the roadside  
          when the wind  
            paused, then  
              up and off  
                again  

    how could we  
  know that  
      great heavy  
uncaring  
    boots  
      would trample  
      us both to  
        broken  
          death?

© By Peter Mardon July 1971.

# Our Tree

My heart swims in the ocean
of your smile.
There are larks in the topmost
branches of our tree, and
caressing the golden trunk,
the jasmine climbs, weaving
her arms in love around
his waist

*

© By Peter Mardon 31/7/1972.

# If Winter Comes

saddened by the visualisation of
colours lost vibrant-warm red

turned to duller brown the
turning of creaking wheel of

time lost moments wailing on the
rust-brown cosmos of uncertainty not

yet forgotten pain-awared still
glowing with the early wonder and

gazing forward to the time that
never comes, wheel turns but

never reaches back into past
tear-river never makes a circle

but ever-onward rich-gold-hued
gems become time-weary-grey and

colours rise and fall as life
itself ebbs and flow not

concerned with the minute moments
strung like hopeless tears upon

a chain reach out and grasp
each passing moment least it dwindle

rust and wither with non-use the
gift is now it is not past

nor yet the future. why wait
for spring when winter is still here
*

© By Peter Mardon 14/7/71.

# War hero

my father
        was a soldier

i want to be
            like him
  a credit to my country
         and
  a source of pride
           to my mother

lanes are not as
   noisy
      as battlefields
       and
  some of the others
           don't want a war

but i made one anyway
   some odd lengths of chain
and
   a piece of
         old pipe some
     tools left
           unused
in the
    shed
a soldier has to use
         his own
           initiative

         one of them cried
         when i hit him
         surely they train

-1-

        them better than
                            that

the last lane on the right
that will be my

headquarters

wish they wouldn't
  leave their metal
    rubbish-bins in
      my headquarters

one of the girls
          screamed
     when
        i raped her

shit! some bastards
     don't know
    how to
     fight

      now
    they're bringing
               guns

and that silly-looking cop
    is
      shouting at me
     as if
      i was a
         criminal

   silly bastards!

-2-

          don't they know
                    there's a war on?

     i'll soon show them
                         i'm no coward
               when it comes to
                              action

                    forward!
                         chains swinging
                         pipe in fist
                         front line
                         attack!

     shit!
               the bloody bullet
               hit me in
                         the chest

                    no matter

     soldiers don't cry

          *

© By Peter Mardon 3/9/71.

# Bush Memories.

1. I have always listened to the song of the trees. They wind their arms around my dreams, and in the rustle of their leaves; I hear the patter of my running feet. "Slow down," they breathe. "You will leave yourself too far behind." So I measure pace with them and found that too, had roots.

2. Sometimes, as I lay hushed in the cool of evening, I pondered if the creek and I were not the same. We intermingled as the sunshine does with air, and taught each other parables.

3. The cows in the paddock remind me of round, brown teapots, full of tea. The comfort is the same. The fields, full of buzzing bees and eucalyptus trees lull me with a secret of their own.

© By Peter Mardon 1971.

# The Victor

Caught within the tangled skein
of sunshine and shade, the
crisp, brown leaves shuddered
beneath the darting rays of
an unrelenting sun.
Summer had overthrown
gentle spring with fearsome roar
of heat, and now rampaged
throughout the tortured land,
burning the blossoms, scorching
the leaves and baring the
staring rocks.
Man could find no refuge
from the torment of his foe,
and ran like a blinded
beast to and fro amid the
wreckage of the sun.
The rocks cracked open in
caustic laughter, knowing as he passed,
that soon he would be as
one of them, his mind
cracked open and seared
beyond recall
but they, the rocks, could mend
again with aching
passage of time, while
man, the master of this
earth, would still remain
a wreck, unhinged by
summer storm.

© By Peter Mardon 17/1/72.

# The V.I.P.

Why they had to send for him
so soon
I don't know

it was not as though
I was a V.I.P.
in fact

I was only paid exactly the same
as all the others
no more no less
perhaps it was because
I had been here
so long

nearly ten years
or was it a hundred?
no I'm sure that

it was not my
endurance
that had made them

so thoughtfully anxious
perhaps
it was because

my dry humour
crackled daily
through the halls

the little nurses
always giggled politely
each time that I told

the same old jokes
that I'd been
telling

for nearly sixty years
or was it
six hundred?

here comes
that pretty little red-head
who always

tucks me in
so comfortably
every night

I'll try to crack
another joke
same old one really

only a crackling
gasp
is coming

never mind
I'll try again
Tonight

when she comes
to tuck me in
that's odd

she's removing all
my sheets
she's washing me down

but it's only
two-thirty
in the afternoon
"Matron" she calls
"he's almost gone
you can

send the
Undertaker
up now."

© By Peter Mardon 24th September, 1971.

# The Ruby

Scarlet stars scintillate
within a crimson sky.
Ah, ruby, what secrets
lie hidden
within your fiery depths?

Who can read your message
blazing red?

Who dare decipher
the hieroglyphics
of your
passionate heart?

Who would defy
that restless sea of blood.
lit by eternal sunsets.
to reach your mystic garden.
where glows the
one red rose
of which all others
are but pale reflections?

Ruby, the sword of Mars,
bathed in crimson carnage,
guards your secret well.

© By Peter Mardon 11th October. 1971.

# Lost

There was no doubt
about it;
the girl was mad.

The ever-watchful eyes
fixed upon his face,
fearful of missing
one movement or
one word.
She had to fill
the vacuum of her mind
with
borrowed things.

Her fingers twined,
untwined;
scratched the harried head.
Something had gone
had vacated
the once golden throne.

She knew no call;
heard only the
steady rhythm
of a brain gone mad.

Somewhere
along its winding track
she had lost her way.

Sounds were jumbled
marbles;
reason was a
coloured clown
dancing to a trombone
out of key.

And no-one heard
the girl who wept within.


©By Peter Mardon 11th October, 1971.

# Suicide

I suppose I could have saved
her; there was no-one else;
only she and I. But, saved
her from what? For what?
She had made her choice.
Who was I, – what right
had I, to try and turn
a decision made after
hours of soulsearching
thought, and then a
gathering together
of courage to see
it through. No I
couldn't do it.
I let her take
the leap; and
cried out as
she fell –
goodluck!

© By Peter Mardon 20th October, 1971.

# Insomuch As Ye Do It Unto The Least of My Brethren …

"Jesus is in our back-yard."
eyes wide,
hands tugging
at mother's sleeve;
"He wants something to eat."

Mother's hands,
and mother's voice,
pushed the child away …
pushed the man away …

"Jesus looks just like his picture,
… the one in you room, mummy."

The old tramp had
no bloody, holy gashes
from crucifixion nails
in his hands …

… no food in his hands …
as he
walked away.

© By Peter Mardon 27th October 1971.

# The New Way

This was never the way it used to be:
smart words and
catchy phrases;
      to drink to death,
and to suffer no remorse
        for empty banter.
Empty life spills out its void;
  the stranger
      in the pub
      becomes a friend
      so swiftly
   that we cannot really
       remember his name;
a name that does not matter.
Call him Mate or Charlie;
    anything will do
       and
   all the girls are birds:
     poor, wingless birds
     that never leave
     the ground.

To find oneself,
      suddenly alone,
      cut off
      from life's reality,
   in a hubbub of

-1-

                    false-sophistication,
                    hiding behind a
                    hundred pseudo-masks,
and
    "Darling, you look lovely!"

the soul's deep sensitivity
shudders into sleep,
            and wakes
            within
    the shut-off, cold seclusion
of
    the mind.


© By Peter Mardon 1st November 1971.

# The Hyacinth of Spring Past

animal-eyes of yellow malevolence
quick-darting, this way, that way
unable to focus,
distrustful, wary,
                       distorting an
already distorted, ugly scene,
into an even more hideous unreality;
that rips
       an unearthly cry from a
       throat – unused to speech.
                *
writhing, turning, trying to
escape the surrounding horror,
       The beast - child- slithers
       His worm -like form
Across the slimy sludge, of the
broken, shattered fragments,
that remain
             to tell a silent
tale of slow, decaying ruin.
                *
something round and heavy
falls beneath the three thumbed
paws,
          he pauses
                  something
of a sweet deep yearning stirs
within his breast
is it love?
can he love? he clutches
his father's rotting head;
             he cannot know

but sits there nursing, crooning,
whimpering his animal-misery
to a parent, dead and gone and
                never known.
                *
time creaks by,
             forgetting the
gloom and stench within the
cave.
               outside, spring
has returned to shower pinks
and golds upon the dappled
green.
               within the cave,
all is dark; sludge and silt;
stench of rotting flesh,
                   and
a lonely child.
                *
              he moves
about, sustaining his beast - body
- with his mother's putrid
corpse;
           nursing his father's head
beside the broken altar; a
sprig of green appears,
               almost convulsing,
the beast-child wails his
          fear beating at his head
             as though
to erase this strange new
image forcing its presence
upon him.

-1-

          \*

      he awakens one morn
to find a greater mystery;
          the green shoot
      has grown,
      become a plant
      and bloomed;
a hyacinth
          gazes back at him
          from its exquisite,
          blue beauty –
          \*

the beast-child, no longer afraid,
wide-eyed and wondering,
              clambers
toward this newcomer to his
              world;
a strange and beautiful fragrance
          assails him;
      no longer does
he see the filth around him,
no more he smells the rot
          of putrid flesh.
\*

the beast-child sits in wonder;
          eyes now-focusing
          upon the hyacinth.
no sound he utters,
no movement makes,
          but fascinated stays
beside his precious trust.

          \*

          time passes, taking
with it the strength and
life
      of the beast-child;
      still smiling,
      eyes focused,
          he dies;
silent and still as his wonder.
      the hyacinth
      droops,
      falls,
      and withers,
      dies away.
        \*

spring has passed.

© By Peter Mardon 11/11/71.

# Destiny

I am a sperm
rushing, swimming
within this marvellous stream
challenging
my many brothers
in the race

faster, faster
only one can win
others must fall
and wither
to unknown nothingness
– halves that can
never be whole

made it!
bliss of union
being
becoming some-one

moving again
– a dark, warm passage
that leads to
life
and further liberty

time has come!
flash of light
heralds
the outside world

warm curved hands
enfold my
new-born beauty
"Joe, how do you want
your egg this morning?
Boiled, poached,
fried or
scrambled?"


© By Peter Mardon 17/11/71.

# Meeting

our eyes met
across
white dunes
of sand

met –
considered.

the eagerness in
your bright orbs
met
the desire in mine.

between us
gleamed the sand –
caustic
and consuming

we knew
the tender plant
could not survive
this
ruthless desert

you passed on by
I
did not
turn around.

© By Peter Mardon 17/11/71.

# Once Motor-Cyclist

To be nailed here
by two legs
to the unmoving
pavement:
                seeing
flashes of freedom
dashing past.

                I once
ran free;
                and now
remember the quick
intake of breath
the press of foot
the bite of wind
upon
                an eager face;

hands strong
and firm
                gripping
the twin bars
that lead
                to freedom
or
                to death.

© By Peter Mardon 14/12/71.

# Inseparable

It took only one glance
at her face
outlined in love
to know
        that lightning
did not matter;
            the white
glaring sheet of face
across the sky.

           I held
her hand
and knew
        that if the
threatening foe
struck one
           it would
be forced
to
        take the other.

© By Peter Mardon 14/12/71.

# This Room

I could not understand
why the cake turned lilac
when we brought it into
this room

this room
that had been coming
for nearly two years

a promise given
and now fulfilled

but it was we
who shared its reward
its quiet serenity
and hushful bliss

he was here
somehow
nearly two years later
he was here

was it him
who gazed from the
little white cupid's eyes
upon the slowly opening
heart of the
pink rose?

were they also
but reflections
of the three candles
that lit
this room
from their realm
among the crystals
of the chandelier?

like crystal
he had been
clear and true
and beautiful

this room
his room
perhaps it is
his reflection

© By Peter Mardon 19/12/71.

# Ego Unalterable

      I began to retrace my
footprints back into time
hoping to do better things
done or not done

      time had almost erased
some prints others remained
bold and clear
though I tried to erase
some prints  prints they would not
go  they kept returning

      memories rushed back
upon my brain bewildering
me with their strange
familiarity

      bitterness regret and
sorrow overwhelmed joy
why is sorrow so much
stronger than joy?
given both sorrow and
joy together the former
engulfs the latter

       arriving at my starting
point I began the forward
journey determined to do
better

       strange how determined
we are upon a given path
we make the same mistakes
suffer the same sorrows
drink the same cup of joy

       I wonder if it is not
the pathway that is fixed
but our own patterns

       we may try to change
circumstances actions or
words
but we ourselves
remain forever
the same
unalterable
SELF.

© By Peter Mardon 1971.

# Norm

    i wonder  
                    as i stand  
beside the window of  
        the dawn  
          what new mad vision  
will fling itself  
at once incomprehensible  
          and yet complete  
to shatter the  
              weary cosmos of  
                my mind

    laughter  
         runs high  
unlit by  
       brother mockery and  
lethargy wins by  
           not  
           even  
           trying

rumblings of  
                      sodden servitude  
     and  
rashness beserk  
call forth the  
unbidden demons of  
               normality

moments   pause   empty  
      reaching out  
             toward  
        the unknown horizon

        today  
        is  
just another  
        ordinary day

© By Peter Mardon 1971.

# Love Is…

Love is the overflowing of one heart into another,
the mingling of two thoughts in single stream,
the running of two pair of feet toward one destination.

Love is a mirror that smiles back a new reflection,
a whispered word, a fond hello, a sad goodbye,
an unaccustomed glow, a weary wait.

Love is a song sung by two voices,
a dark room filled with light, not knowing, and not caring
why,
just is,
a solitary moment – not alone.

Love is the momentary doubt, the wince of pain,
the soaring of a bird,
a sweet refrain.

Love is a Winter's day as warm as Spring,
a city street alive with flowers,
love-songs pouring forth from traffic's roar.

Love is a Sunday full of woe,
Monday bliss, a quick and eager touch,
forever kiss.

Love is a television programme,
neither share,
the clatter of a milk-cart,
cat's miaow.

-1-

Love is four hundred times "I miss you",
friends abused,
new meaning to some long forgotten words.

Love is a tender steak, burnt black,
and coffee cold,
a card all-crumpled from too often touch.

Love is a train that is missed,
a ticket never used,
grass stains and wind-swept hair
and such.

Love is half-finished words,
and promises not kept,
a night that turns to dawn,
a gift of tears.

Love is the sharing of a dream,
a shattered hope,
walking in the rain
not feeling wet.

Love is the moment of delight,
the sense of Spring,
the yearning to be near,
and everything.

© By Peter Mardon 1971.

# You Came Into My Life

Like a summer morn
you breathed life
into my rattling
bones.

Heavy with fragrance
you tore apart
the palings of
my desert fence
and
        drenched the air
with love.

Come spring
            come summer
birds will nest again

and in the autumn
we shall sit beneath
the golden trees
counting the
leaves
       with love.

Winter shall find us
warm
close-knit.
          as a flower is
one
      in perfume and petal.

© By Peter Mardon 1971.

# YOU, I LOVE

Beside the pool
deep, dark, and shadow-green,
I see your eyes
-liquid stars
beaming love.

My heart melts
with love for you.

like a slim wraith
deep, dark, unfathomable,
you glide away.

My heart, my love,
swims after you,
longing to enfold,
bestow a love
more deep, more dark,
more unfathomable
than the pool
of shadow-green.

© By Peter Mardon 1971.

# Awakening

You were waiting for me
in all your myriad forms
        unseen
        unknown
I was unaware
            of your presence
until your multi-colours
wound around
        my mind
in cluttered
        confusion.

solitary sounds were
        visible
at the moment of
        impact

somewhere far above
bells began
        to ring

awakening is not easy

          the patchwork quilt
that covered
          my nakedness
no longer had use or
          purpose
something
     was
          …missing.

awareness leapt upon me
      with
        triumphant shout
      and
      buried dead things
in the past
        of oblivion.

© By Peter Mardon 1971.

# The Sacrifice

Last night I lay upon my bed;
My peace of mind had swiftly fled.
A premonition hovered where
The door was open to despair.

I heard the drumming of my heart;
The awful, pregnant moment start.
The waiting vacuum filled with fear
As Something horrid hovered near.

My eyes could only see the night,
And darkness but increased my fright.
Rising, screaming, hands ashake,
I tried the evil spell to break.

But, though I tried, I could not pray,
My lips but blasphemy could say.
Within the distance Something died,
And Something for its mate now cried.

The wings of Satan wrapped me round,
And with His hatred was I crowned.
"Come on, come on," a chorus wailed,
And on a cross I was impaled.

Oh, sudden horror! Why awake?
Did conscience from its dreaming break?
The cauldron bubbled, foul the brew;
Yet my torment was not through.

A thousand disembodied hands
Bore me over shifting sands
I watched great empires rise and fall,
Nothing e'er remained at all,

-1-

Excepting Satan's empire bright;
The furnace kept it full of light.
But pits there were, as dark as night,
And headlong down I took my flight.

I came to rest within a pool;
They crowned me there – the Never Fool.
A bull-frog croaked, and gave me pause
To wonder at my living cause.

The air grew hushed, and soft the wind
Whispered, "Friend, you have not sinned.
But every age must have its day,
And Scapegoat for its sins must pay."

I wept and pleaded, "But why me?"
Answer said, "You're Effigy!"
With sodden sorrow did I weep,
And tried my sanity to keep.

But, up again, upon the cross,
They carried me, the sands across,
Until we reached an awful place,
Not ever seen by human race.

A mighty pyre was waiting there;
I screamed, but no-one seemed to care.
They cast me high upon the stack,
Then, swift the flames went crackle-crack!

It seemed my final end had come;
But had they solved the final sum?
The tears were bitter to my taste
As Answer answered, "No, 'tis waste!"

© By Peter Mardon 1971.

# Waiting Time to Come

Why can't we be
like
      the fig-leaved, when
      not seen
by ancient eyes

not forced or fallen,
pills
      numerous and bottles
      not empty
say, can't we be

like
      nobody, with
nixed
      eye-balls yearning
      away to
another day: years
          faded
                to
                nothing

© By Peter Mardon 1971.

# Sanctuary

No point in telling her to
clean the damn thing. Why
disturb the moths, dust,
insects – refugees seeking
shelter in a safety/danger
zone of flickering light/life?

Anyway, the only time that it
flecks my eye is when I'm in
my own wet shield of trying–
to–escape the eternal encroach–
ment of talcum-powder, tooth–
paste, spray and bathroom rack.

Squizzing the wisdom of the bugs,
my own vague threads intermingle
with their wise invulnerability;
flip across and beat my drum of
human–head–denial, and lap the
waterway of free content

A honeymoon of thoughts buzzes
sweet and mad and true: nectar
I can ken and breathe. Out there,
the manic chatter beats a hope–
less tattoo on my door; too many
words – not enough to say;
gibble-gabble of a turkeyed-world.

We are undisturbed – the insects
and I. the distance between is
far too wide for them to reach
us now. Think I'll bury my head
beneath the quiet folds of my
safety/danger zone and pretend
that I am drowned.

© By Peter Mardon 1971.

# The Sound of Heaven

The sound of heaven is in the wind,
Behold! The white Dove flying!
There is no winner; none have sinned;
There is no fear of dying.

The scarlet plume lies in the dust;
Behold! the white flag flying!
There is no Famine, none eat crust;
There is no sound of crying.

The Silver sword is sheathed at last;
Behold! The grass is green!
There is no darkened shadows cast;
There is no foe unseen.

The Prince of Peace now wears the Crown;
Behold! his robe is white!
There is no fear of falling down;
There is no Cause but Right.

The song of freedon all may sing;
Behold! Eternal Sun!
There is no bird without a wing,
There's hope for everyone.

The pure white blossom blooms again;
   Behold! sweet perfume rare!
There is no burden now for men;
   There is peace everywhere.

Now shines the lovely face of God;
   Behold! The healing kiss!
Now rests the ever-chastening rod;
   And all is hallowed bliss.

© By Peter Mardon 28/10/68

## For Love Eternal

Eternal love, we wear thee as a crown!
Love never dims; this is thy lovely
   secret, that only lovers know.

We thank thee, love, that thou hast
   blest us both; and hand in hand
   shall we bear thee as our
holy crown throughout eternity.

© By Peter Mardon 11/9/68

# Cosmic Conversation

What says the earth
to the distant star?

glimmer of reflected light
gratitude in lovers' eyes
a sharing in the
cosmic birth
and death;

and through the
million-light-year-eyes
of far Andromeda
– a unified refulgence.

© By Peter Mardon 1971.

# The Love Star

Words
like lonely stars
whirl around their
galactic brain;
part of a unity,
yet total in themselves.

Catching
one star,
I gazed deep;
the nucleus hidden
within a tangled
mess of
refuse flung from
other passing
stars;
atoms whirling free.

Spinning away
on its
zig-zag path,
the love star
struck me
between eyes,
brain unscathed;

weaving its
flotsam tail
like a floating comet
around the
galactic course.

© By Peter Mardon 1972.

# In The Midst…

In the midst of the flame of
this world, you stand;
the answer to every question
that forms within the tunnel of
my mind.

No other
reality, except you; you motivate
my actions, stimulate my
thoughts, fulfil my dreams.

For you I would weave the web
of life … gather the stars to
build your house …

© By Peter Mardon 1972.

# The Downpour-Flood

In a city street the water
coloured brown was washing
the faces of the windows
kissing the doors of cars and
ripple-laughing round the
knees of city-downpour people;
a river flowed in Elizabeth
Street mocking Summer's smile
with tears of laughing rain
and proving to a race of
man-supreme that clouds
still have a say.

© By Peter Mardon 18/2/72.

# The Silence

There was silence
in the town
after
the old man
died.

The wind dropped
branches ceased their shuffle,
and cattle
no longer bellowed.

During the silence,
a child was born
and even he
refused
to cry.

The townfolk wondered
what had caused
the silence.
Some thought that
the town
must be cursed
because
it had let
the old man
die.

No-one had known
who the old man was.
He had wandered
into town
with empty hands

-1-

and empty belly,
asking only
for work
to earn some food.

But no-one
gave him
either work or food,

and so
he died
alone
in a gully grave;

and
there was silence
in the town
after
the old man
died …

© By Peter Mardon 7th January 1972.

# Past Thoughts

(1)
When we meet I shall know you at once.
Our smiles will blend to form an island
which only those who truly love can reach.
And in the morning we shall again be
strangers, lost upon a never-ending
track of heart-unrest.

(2)
There are traces in the sand of lost seasons.
The wind brushes them aside for the moment of
farewell; and whispers them again in distant
places set about with ruins, where weeds grow
wild, watered with wasted tears.

(3)
Do not look for me amid the gardens of the
world. The hours are too long to wait for
buds to bloom. Rather, seek me in the desert
where the sand can form a million different
patterns in one day.

(4)
Language is a useless vehicle upon which
no man of thought can ride. A smile, a glance,
a touch can offer more, and paint a truer
portrait. Bind up your words in books
and bury them, before they bury you.

(5)
I used to search for truth among the litter-cans and trees. The pain of finding was too great, so I leapt upon the horse of illusion, and chattered on about philosophy.

(6)
I live in two houses; one I share with you; the other I hardly dare share with myself. The pictures on the walls are made of clay; they crumble and distort with every breath. Outside, the trees and bushes turn away and shudder with their own peculiar thoughts.

(7)
I found you hidden in a curl of leaves. Your pattern, partly-formed, had a strange perfection in its imperfection. My mind began to shatter and could not hold the vision. In your wisdom, you moved away; leaving me whole though quite unsatisfied.

© By Peter Mardon 30th March, 1972.

# Thoughts of Evermore

(1)
When we meet I shall know you at once;
for you are the mirror of my thoughts, the
memory I left behind when love first bloomed.
For you I shall sing the song of the morning,
and in its rustle shall return the Spring.

(2)
Tender are the blossoms that spill their magic
forth from your lips. In the circle of light is
found the flash of freedom; but in its shadow
is hid the secret of your return.

(3)
Turn not away from destiny's bitter stream. We
walked this way before, when summer was a child,
and found rainbow lollies hidden in its breast.
Perhaps a pot of gold awaits us now.

(4)
There are no more walks among the stars.
See how the sky weeps her jewels away, and
turns to meet a season new as life. Creation
kills to recreate, and birth is ever-restless as
the storm.

(5)
Count not the times we said goodbye. Rather let
us learn a new hello. There are fallen leaves that
yearn toward the earth. They dig a shallow grave.
Leap with me toward our star's rebirth.

-1-

(6)
Honey is as sweet as the flower's tender kiss,
but your kiss excels in sweetness and in truth.
For you I shall level mountains, fill valleys
full of dreams, and wear your smile before
my eyes, remembering our love.

(7)
Wait for me upon the hill of Dawn. When
sunset comes, I shall ride the glowing sun
the circle round, to rise again and kiss
you as you stand. Upon your hair shall
I alight turning it to gold and rose, and
Whispering 'I love you, evermore'.

© By Peter Mardon 31/03/72.

# Thoughts, Of Love

(1)
When we meet I shall know you at once.
We shall sit beneath the trees and see the
world begin. Listen! The birds have
learned a new song, to herald the world's
birth and our meeting.

(2)
The breeze is cool against your face, and
the grass is newly-painted green. Our hearts
are green again and unfold toward a
new beginning.

(3)
The willow wears a thousand secrets. Who
can decipher the message carved upon her
ancient breast? Let a man stand beneath
her curtains of green and he shall know it
all. But when he moves away from her
embrace, the sunlight scorches and turns
it all to dust.

(4)
My heart is a playground for your love.
Tread gently upon the golden strings and they
Will sing you a song to remember when
There is no more you or me. We are
But passing thoughts in the eternal stream
of love.

(5)
The white bird sails across the mirrored lake. He bears a message of peace to come, but cannot find a place to set it free. Rough hands warn whiteness not to pause. They are not ready yet for his descent.

(6)
When I am gone, my love shall still be seen. Look amid the sticks and stones that litter every path. See the tiny white flowers shining like silver stars that twinkle in-between. They are the many ways I love you.

(7)
Let us take the journey of the clouds. White and high and free. Snowball ourselves across the dappled blue. Then fall like gentle rain to kiss the earth which brought us forth, and takes us back again.

© By Peter Mardon 1/4/72.

# Thoughts
# You & I, Toward Eternity

1
The silence of the night does not worry us
with its restful labour. In its shadows, images
are lost and new ones can begin. The quiet of
our souls is never known until we meet upon
the borderland of dreams.

2
A refugee from the dark is knocking on our
door. Someone has lost his pain, and life has
become intolerable. Against a colourless sky,
no birds can fly.

3
Read to me from the pages of an Autumn leaf,
and I shall count the seasons on my hand. Know
that the pale eyes of Winter have for their pupils,
the twin promises of Spring. Somewhere, along the
back road of Summer, a child is singing.

4
The bird cannot find its nest, and circles
eternally in old/new spirals made of thought.
A trumpet sounds,
and flocks of geese descend, leaving behind
some grey, more blue, one gold. They count the
marshes with their beaks and drain the empty cup.

5
Substance is the enemy of soul. No man can
see the road through human eyes. When we leave
the shore, we hear the splash of the oar, but we
cannot understand the song of the sea.

-1-

6
Walk with me through the fields of never-been. There is something hidden there that we both must see and know; but the knowing is different for both of us.

7
When I was born, another person died. Someone smiled for me and cried for him. The balance of the scales is held within the future of the wind.

8
Do not try to tell me where the hour-hand
Rests. At midnight, the sun is still as bright.
At midday, the stars still move, bathed in beauty. They cannot see the clock upon your shelf. I travel with the sun and stars.

9
Let us count the colours of the butterfly. She wears her smile in the patterns, and traces her joy from leaf to flower and back again. Sunshine and shade are both her home; she shares her wealth with a watchful world.

10
The youth, born in chains of time, leapt toward
The stars. He found himself lying beneath a dying tree. The tree had been dying for a hundred years, the youth for ten. They added the sum, subtracted their weight, and found a multitude of stones.

11
Teach me only to know your name. Between us stands a world of weight. The touch of your hand is light enough to travel the distance, and the longing in my heart sufficient source. Our loneliness stretches from East to West, but does not rise nor set. It is the blue of the sky, the green of the grass, and upon its arc, the seasons spin.   -2-

12
Angels have no need of wings. Being eternal,
time cannot defeat their ways. Therefore, they
may crawl and still achieve their aim. But, we
who are bound by time, have need to make wings.
Why then, is the ascent so small?

13
There is no more going down of the sun; no more
a moon that lights a lover's eyes. Time has destroyed
our mysteries and left us in a barren land where
only the first sum is known. We have returned to
our first day at school, where one and one are
always two.

14
Your face, lost against the waiting sky has absorbed
into its contours, the silence of the trees.
The grass whispers to the stones, against which
my foot trembles, and I find myself streaming out in
tears across a famished land.

15
If I were Mister God, I would paint the sky in
green, alter the tone of sunrise, and set it in a field.
Fishes would walk and talk, and stars would laugh;
Trees grow upside down, and time retreat. But you
would remain the same.

16
Outside the labyrinth of life, the fields are
grey. They wait for children to come and paint their
dreams. The unborn blades of grass drink patience
with their tears, and love sits mourning for what
might not come.

-3-

17
Lines and angles intersect our grief. Too sharp
and clear, they shout and rage against the contours
of our warm. Let us retire to smooth, round boulders;
bury ourselves within the comfort of the sand; and
watch the golden circle of our sun.

18
We breathe and think the thoughts of other men, and
measure our success by others' tears. Let us leap the
boundary, spread a net, and fill the vase with flowers
not yet known. There is a garden waiting to be sown.

19
The rhythm of our lives has its secret beneath the
weightless rocks that time has borne. The grass we
crush beneath our feet quivers with the knowledge,
and writes its epitaph upon the tombstone of our
mind.

20
Don't mourn that the Old Man has gone. He does not
know. Grant Him the immunity from man he would
have wished.
His breath was wasted and his song unheard.
The dying cannot hear the living or the dead.

21
Sometimes, I am more me than you. At other times,
I am definitely you. When the star cuts the night
with its silence, our dreams connect.

© By Peter Mardon 2/5/72.

# Mind-Thoughts

(1) In the shaft of light, I caught a glimpse of your shadow. Something
reached out and struck me from behind. I found myself bathed in
nothingness. You had gone from before me.

*

(2) In the pause before the dawn, a new thought stole into our garden;
The golden seed hidden in a maze of marigolds. Now we must be careful
where we tread.

*

(3) The ants have found a new hiding-place. The scramble to and fro,
oblivious to the old. One walked over a cousin's grave, but kept on writing
stories for a future generation, unaware that the tale had already been told.

*

(4) We stand before the feast of seasons, hands cupped to catch a fleeting
glance. What if the wheel should shift … reality force us forth into the
season of despair? Could we still hold hands and smile?

*

(5) The peacocks are serenading the restless sun. They wear rubies in
Their eyes for the lost time, hoping the sun will lift them up, they fail
to see the blade of corn.

*

(6) In the reflection of the pool, old men are washing themselves. They cannot wait
for the third bell to ring. To them it is always morning.

*

(7) Before the mystery of the road we are helpless. The song of the crickets,
full of wisdom, is incomprehensible to the mind of man; and the bees continually
blend their honey as they sing.

*

(1) There is a hope in death that the timeless never know. A distant
shore moves shadows to its beat. Over and over, the drummer
kills the drum, but the song had moved to cycles of its own.

*

(2) The season of the fool has reached the house. Windows smile
and shatter silent glass. An unhinged door makes gestures at the
moon, and relevance has lost its solemn theme.

© By Peter Mardon 3/5/72 – 5/5/72.

# The Final Wisdom

Angels are beings
dressed in clouds
who weep
         to see
the follies of man.

      Man's stupidity
curses the rain,
            which
is
the sustainer of life.

The Universe keeps
watch.
         decreeing
that
    man must perish;
clouds remain.
Where then is Wisdom?
         The eye of God
is sharp,
     and
the eye of man
         blind.

© By Peter Mardon 15th February 1972.

# Cabbage

I spoke of roses to a fool;
he only spoke of kings.
The frog retreated to his pool
and croaked of other things.

A cabbage in my garden grew;
she wore a dress of green;
but she insisted it was blue,
else it had never been.

The fool I met again one day,
a crown upon his head;
the crown it was a cabbage gay;
"Now I am king!" he said.

The frog croaked out, "The pool is dry!"
The fool peered in to see;
but when he found the water high,
said, "Ho, this cannot be!

The frog has said the water's gone,
so I'll not drown, you see."
And so he stepped the water on,
and sank abysmally.

But as I wandered past that spot,
I saw a flash of green;
it was a cabbage in a pot,
floating so serene.

"I am a cabbage, did she say,
"My colour is still blue!"
I pondered as I walked away,
and thought, "Why, yes! That's true!"

© By Peter Mardon 1972.

# The Shadow

The man's shadow
followed him
        all the days
        of his life,
until
    his last hour.
           Perceiving
that the man was
about to die,
        the shadow
untangled itself
from the man,
        and hid itself
within the room's
darkened drapes.

The body buried,
widow mourned,
        children cried;
and
    the shadow screamed
    to find itself
trapped forever
within
    darkened drapes.

© By Peter Mardon 27/1/72.

# Child of Sorrow

The avalanche of the time
engulfed
        his seven years
burning a picture
           full
     of tragic fire.

His eyes were
aged with sorrow
           and
loneliness
       sat upon his
       brow,
           picking
the few remaining crumbs

from
        a mind grown far
        beyond its years.
we wondered
           if anyone
           could ever
enter that
           childhood desolation
to
       bring him back again.

© By Peter Mardon 26/1/72.

# The Apple of Deliverance

The tree grew out of
the morning
         with
              hardly a question
to bind in grey
its
      iridescent trunk.

          White petals
kissed the air
whispering secrets of
flower-love.

Green the foliage,
spelling out
          its welcome
to velvet-soft touch
of time's bird of truth.

Discord
jangled her rude warning,
impinging a
          different chord
upon the harmonic
song of joy.

                Pink and gold,  
blue and black  
struck their colours forth  
to abolish the  
                foul intruder;  
                        but  
the fruition of time  
brought forth  
                an apple,  
banishing discord  
and  
        weaving  
        a more gently harmony  
with  
        the total truth.

© By Peter Mardon 25/1/72.

# Message of the Black Dove

I am the black dove,
that cried, "War. war!"
then drunk with
bitter blood,
        cry "Peace!"

My wings have fanned the flames of
hatred,
passion, lust;

I have watched man
walk a million roads,
and turn
to dust.

Ride on!
There is still one road
        to know.

The black sabbath
still hangs
across the sky:
        and man
has taught himself
a million
ways to die.

Ride on!
There is still one road
        to know.

-1-

Love has lost itself
amongst the ashes;
              and phoenix
cannot breathe.
Man unearths a
              dying theory
that the children
can believe.

Ride on!
There is still one road
              to know.

Stars scatter light
that time can eat;
man leaps
toward the stars
              turns victory
              to defeat.

Ride on!
There is still one road
              to know.

I am the black dove,
that cried, "War. war!"
then drunk with
bitter blood,
              cry "Peace!"

© By Peter Mardon 18/1/72.

# The Mystic Boy

Down the everlasting stream
of Rapture's first impassioned dream,
he drifts, with pure, white sails unfurled;
and in his hands, he holds the world;
the mystic boy, with shining eyes,
guides the way to Paradise.
He sees the everlasting sun
arise, and call, "The race is run!"
He sees the everlasting moon
arise, and sing another tune.
So still and calm the boy now stands,
the world at rest within his hands.
He wears the crown of mystic light
upon his hair of deepest night;
his eyes so shining and so clear
like glittering diamonds bright appear;
and o'er his shoulders strong and proud,
is flung a mantle like a cloud
of rich dark hues, all-shot with gleams
of dancing stars like raptured dreams.
His skin, like alabaster rare
lends beauteous contrast to his hair.
Not yet a man, but still a youth,
with shining eyes aglowwith truth,
he steers his course unswerved and true:
a course that's known to but a few.
A patient smile upon his lips,
and graceful curve of thigh and hips;
he, never weary, wends his way
toward the newborn, waiting day.
The longest day is closing now;
the last leaf falls from golden bough;
the weary exile soon shall end
as mystic boy shall take the bend
that lies beyond his eyes keen gaze;
then, o'er the all, shall fall the rays

of Ennell's dawning, pure and bright,
and he shall bathe in Ennell's light.
The ransomed ones will weep for joy
to see the lovely mystic boy;
the garden will in triumph bloom
and kiss the air with sweet perfume;
the world will wake with joyous shout,
and gone fore'er are fear and doubt.
The Ennling's curse shall fade away
as mystic boy reveals the day.
An arc of iridecent beams
reflects in Ennell's crystal streams;
and music, sweeter than a bird,
throughout the ransomed land is heard.
all this the mystic boy well knows,
As down the raptured stream he flows:
his vessel bound for gloryland
the world's bright orb within his hand.
He sometimes sings a ballad so sweet,
He sings, "My love and I shall meet."
And overhead, the sound of wings
is heard to flutter as he sings
the unknown bird still flies up high
and watches all, with knowing eye.
"Come home! Come home!" is in his song,
"With me, beloved, you belong!"
Their songs become a duet fair
resplendent on the dewy air.
And thus, toward his destiny
the mystic boy sails pure and free.
So, as he nears his journey's end,
kaleidoscopes within him blend;
all time is held within his eyes;
now shed at last the false disguise.
All that was, and ever is,
the crown and sceptre, all are his;
so truth and beauty now are shown
as mystic boy ascends his throne.

© By Peter Mardon 1972.

# Bus-Riders Nine

The bus spilled out its load
into the desert.

Two planted seeds
and watched them grow.

One sang of God
and warbled ancient hymns.

Another leapt upon the rocks
and tried to touch the stars.

The fifth one
went to find another bus.

Three joined hands
and pledged
eternal Brotherhood.

The last one
stopped to thank the weary bus.

© By Peter Mardon 25/1/72.

# Angel

I saw her coming to me
through the fields of lilacs
twin lilacs shining in her eyes
and lilacs in her hands

for me alone?

Crystalline her hair and
crystals were her eyes
shining like the twin stars
of Gemini

for me alone?

Like snow upon her forehead
clear and pure
her hands like snow
so cool and white
reaching … reaching …

for me alone?

My arms reached out
to clasp her

she drifted through
beyond me

scented of lilacs
shimmer of crystal
cool of snow

ringing a little, silver bell.

© By Peter Mardon 1972.

# The Youth

He was as slender as a sapling,
yet seemed to have a strength
and speed far beyond his years.

He ran past the quicksands of youth,
Skimming over doubt and delusion,
And claimed the truth as his inheritance.

Always with a song upon his lips,
he scattered seeds of Spring
throughout our Winter-land.

Morning caught him running, wild and free;
the noonday sun lay hidden in his smile,
and evening made a nest within his hair.

Yet, he vanished from among us, leaving
a sigh upon the evening breeze, and questions
like forget-me-nots, nodding in the sun.

© By Peter Mardon 28/1/72.

# The Tears of Time

The boy of the crystal eyes,
hour-glass full of sand,
sprinkled seeds of Time
throughout the Stars

weaving them into seasons,
times and death,
wearing his own sweet smile
like an everlasting Song of Joy.

He watched
while silver chains
encircled his new-born world,
and heard the cry
of wonder and of pain.

His crystal eyes watched Man
with measures step
eat and breathe
to beat of drum
that had its cause from seed.

He felt the suffocation,
knew the sorrow of a Son;

then swiftly smashed
his hour-glass
that drank too many tears.

© By Peter Mardon 14/1/72.

# Aries Memory

It rests like a great black
rock upon its cloak of golden sand
while overhead, the sky burnished
with the brilliant sun of Mars.

Before it rolls the deep blue sea,
eternal and unchanging.

Surrounding the castle, the land
daunts any soul – so barren, lifeless
and full of crumbling rocks.

But it was here I loved to roam,
searching under rocks for strange
creatures with which to play;

and leaping from crag to crag like
any young and eager deer.

© By Peter Mardon 22nd July 1972.

# The Travellers

The cave
engulfed by fire
told a saga yet to come
of a man and boy
walking
from Eternity to Infinity.

They bore upon their shoulders
the world's weight
and future Call;

not shrinking from the fire
or cave as dark as death.

Outside,
the seasons spun
upon a wheel of change;

and Time up-ended
mocked at man's endeavour,

yet shone like crystal droplets
from the eyes
of a man and boy.

© By Peter Mardon 28.1.1972.

# The Stallions

Too hard to tame them; the wild
stallions of my mind. If I could
find their shadowed origin, being
at the beginning, maybe they could
be dislodged, turned to a new direction.

There they could trample other signposts,
plough other grounds with their steely
hooves of fire;

        and the corner of
my eye would only need reflect the
cloud-burst of destruction,
storming around their sweat-oiled
bodies,

        as I re-order the upturned
clods of my own unjointed mind.

© By Peter Mardon 1 February 1972.

# Time

Beyond the mystery of the moon,
the universe sighed,
shedding shivers of silver
through her starry domain.

Where was the boy
who
with questions in his eyes,
had caused the stars to spin,
the moon to rise
and made the oceans flow?

Had he grown weary of the Game?
Or was he caught somewhere
amid the tangled skein
unable to free himself?

No;
beside a steady sea-shore,
strewn with
multi-coloured shells,
sat the boy,
and hour-glass in his hand,
a smile upon his lips.

He filled the glass with sand …

© By Peter Mardon 13.1.1972.

# Dementia

A madman runs to and from
in the now deserted street;
children have been gathered in,
doors bolted, minds closed.
"feed the poor! feed the poor!"
the madman yells.
A child begins to whimper;
mother stuffs a lolly in …
a small price for such blessed peace.

Someone rings the cops;
"There's a madman running loose."
Cop finished his sandwich,
drinks his cup of brew.
Law and Order must be enforced.
"What would these mugs do
if there were no cops."

Still the madman rages up and down
the street, "feed the poor! feed the poor!"
Curious eyes watch from safe enclosures;
what a sight the man is!
unkempt, unclean, unfit
for civilized society.
Men like him should be locked away.

Police-sirens' wail joins in
a crazy duet with the madman's wail.
He runs from door to door,
beating, scratching, hammering
until his bony fists are bloody-raw,
as bloody-raw as his desperate cry,

"feed the poor! feed the poor"
The doors stand firm and mute.

The madman zig-zags across
the silent street, frothing now,
his eyes glazed, unseeing.
Round the corner speeds the cop,
his car at fever-pitch;
Zig-zags the madman,
Skid and screech, a sickening thud.
the madman drinks his own blood,
gurgling still,
"feed the poor! feed the poor!"

"Best thing that could have happened,"
everyone agreed.
"A man like that is better off dead."

It took a little while to clean up
the bloody mess,
write the report,
fill in the eager-eyed reporters …

but the little girl who lay
in a near-delirium of starvation,
awaiting the return of her
darling daddy,
took a little longer to die.

© By Peter Mardon 20th September 1971.

# The Golden Girl

The sun illuminated her golden hair
with such a lucernal beauty,
                that the young man
                scarcely noticed
the old man leaning on her arm
like a fragile, silver thread.

The young man paused,
        his eyes in love;
    he brought her smiles
    and dainty words;
    flowers;
        then a ring.

She received them all,
              returned his kiss;
    said, "Grandfather, dear, please
        bless us."
    In silvery silence he watched them wed.

The young man wondered
why the old man
        never smiled.

They buried his ninety-two years
with him in a
        lonely grave.

The young man and his golden bride
    made happiness their friend;
but
        twenty-five years
        caused them to
leave their home.

The neighbours rattled
        of the man
    who was fifty
    and his bride
        still twenty-one.

They moved around;
    not waiting for
    the tongues
    to chatter.

At seventy he leaned upon her arm;
at ninety-two
        he lost his way of speech.

The sun illuminated her golden hair
with such lucernal beauty,
        that the young man
        scarcely noticed
    the old man …

© By Peter Mardon 13th October 1971.

# Man

Who are you?

I am a speck of animated dust,
eating myself in order to survive.

Where are you from?

From yesterday, today, tomorrow
and forever.

Why did you come?

To find myself, hidden in my
own reflected light.

Where are you going?

Round and round, up and down,
back and forth, forever.

© By Peter Mardon 16th November 1971.

# Life-Between

dawn comes but once
in each man's life
and evening closes down

his shutters with sure
finality day spins
her spell

of sun and shade, of leaf
and wind and tree and
other things beside

let us enjoy the solace
of this something-
in-between

© By Peter Mardon 1972.

# Journey with Death

I took a walk along the road with Death yesterday.
He took me past the dreaming-cave where Night used to play.
I saw the barren reaches, where the nightmares love to run,
And I saw the weary eyes gazing blindly at the sun.

I heard an Angel singing of the time that used to be,
And the whisper of the innocent made ripples in the sea.
I tried to keep my soul alive, but Death replied with laugh,
And when I faltered on the way, he struck me with his staff.

There was no pity in his eyes, nor sorrow in his glance,
His only wisdom was to watch the night's revolving dance.
He cast me on a nightmare that was terrible to see;
I didn't know where I would go, to set my poor soul free.

A hundred haggard witches, with cackles, watched my flight,
As the nightmare galloped onward through the screaming, gaping night.
I tried to pray, but prayer could not, within that place, be heard.
It seemed that I, the wrath of God, forever had incurred.

For, never did it seem, could I e'er dismount my steed,
As he galloped ever onward with swift, increasing speed.
I felt the rain upon my face, but it was raining blood,
And the barren land beneath the hooves, was horrid, writhing mud.

The sky was black, and evil eyes above now watched the scene,
As, with a cry, the horse and I, leapt o'ver a great ravine.
I knew that I could not return; too wide that awful gap.
And the I heard a sickly sound – a steady rap! tap! tap!

-1-

I did not know what made the sound, but all my senses froze,
As there before my tortured gaze, all horrid, Death arose.
I heard the screams of others lost, but no-one could I see.
I only knew the end was near, with awful certainty.

Stark Horror opened wide his jaws, and bloody stench was all,
And then I felt myself descend beneath the screaming pall.
I seemed to hear my poor soul scream, and then Myself was gone;
And everywhere, without a care, the world just rumbled on.

© By Peter Mardon 1971.

# To Go Onward; Or To Where?

To take the proffered hand; not sure of which.
The turmoil of a journey, here or there.
Moments, strung like beads upon a chain;
seemingly one, yet separate and alone.

The past still breezes round an ear grown cold;
perhaps too many sounds have uttered here.
A half-viewed road, vague memories or where;
and some-one whom the name has left behind.

Can tears reach out and clear the cluttered path?
Too many vague farewells, too many nows.
The world will always turn its side-drift way,
and man must fall a victim to its play.

What can we say to make the pattern clear?
Perhaps no piece remains to fill the place;
The jig-saw has no end, no sense of rhyme,
And we are but illusions of the storm.

© By Peter Mardon 1st November 1971.

# Earthbound

I am the weeping willow that gazes forever
into the pool of biter compromise, catching
only reflections and never the substance
real. Waiting hoping for swallows in
the Spring, but knowing that the silent
swan will always pass me by, the crown
of darkness gleaming on the royal brow.

*

Ah, God! I weep, praying constantly that
tears will wash away the aching film of
blindness that haunts my every dream.
See how the breeze stirs my many arms,
Lifting them, waving them, while I in
quiet terror try to fly, aware always
of the unbreakable chains that bind me
to the ground.

*

Smile, sky, smile! Why so blue?
Your intangible arms embrace a million wings.
Weep, why weep? Your myriad eyes gaze
down on tortured things, and know that
you forever dwell within without.

*

I am the weeping Willow. Pity me.
Yet, no; not pity. Rather, send me
one small, white feather to catch in
empty arms, awaking hope; to strive,
to fly the shining, silver highway of
the sky.

*

For me shall it become all things, and
upon its light the world will rise to
greet my coming day; the song unsung
shall find its hidden chord; and in the
marble hand of time the bowl will break,
freeing, scattering the secret flowers
that lit my former way.

© By Peter Mardon 4th October 1971.

# Adam's Luck

Like an apple, gleaming red,
upon a tree,
she was to me
temptation;

out of reach,
not out of sight;

I crossed the barrier
that night;
and took one sweet, forbidden bite;

grew dizzy with elation.

I kicked the warning
signal down,
in apple-juice I'd
gladly drown,

like Adam
on creation

But, just as he,
when, from the tree,
plucked forbidden fruit,

took one bite
of sheer delight,
and felt the master's boot.

© By Peter Mardon 28th October 1971.

# The Bringer of Love

Dark pain has left my heart;
the bringer of love is here,
whose form is the earth-bubble sphere,
the sun and the moon mixing mirth;
snow-murmurings welcome his touch,
for his are the fingers that cool.
Dark pain has left my heart.

The ocean of bliss is unbound;
the bringer of love is here,
whose eyes are a lessening tear,
that kiss-balm the pain-raging dearth;
the white-wonder of winter is gone,
for his are the fingers that soothe.
The ocean of bliss is unbound.

Earth wakens to sing a new song;
the bringer of love is here,
whose voice, like time's bell, ringing clear
arouses each seed to its birth;
spring rises from winter's snow-spell,
for his are the fingers that weave.
Earth wakens to sing a new song.

© By Peter Mardon 8th November 1971.

# The Reflection

In the village
the boy walked alone
– something to do with
the rags that he wore
and the name that
he bore.

But the river was free
and the water clear.
Here the boy rested on
the river-bank and gazing
into the water below
he saw his own reflection
mirrored twice.

He sat there in his rags,
while his other self wore
lordly clothes and mocking smile. Bitterly the boy
reached out, and flung
the other one who mocked

down beneath the river's
cloak, breaking the mirrored
surface, and the law.
The village Lord, whose son
had been drowned, sentenced
the boy to death–
and thus lost twins.

© By Peter Mardon 10th January 1972.

# Rain

It was mid-summer
but the rain still fell.

Up in the mountain
an old man
was telling tales
of past and present and future,

weaving them together
like a multi-coloured scarf
of strange design;
a day a stitch,
a name a thread;

while in the corner of his room
a boy cried.
He was a story too, but no-one knew his name.
His colour was green
and he wore sugar-plums
in his hair.

Spring had passed,
Summer was king,
but the boy's sweet rain
still fell …

© By Peter Mardon 14.1.1972.

# The Eternal One

Before the world began:
before even chaos:
he was the darkness that hovered over the deep;
the unbridled wind that howled throughout the cosmos.
In some distant, unlit recess of time
his dark soul brooded ...
brooded ... brooded ...
until his fierce, wild song burst forth,
causing the universe to shudder into existence.

His was the rebellious spirit let loose
within the molten lava,
the earth's deep fissures tearing wide,
the swirling ocean's roar.
In gigantic monsters he trod the land,
until extinction was their lot.

He was the ancient warrior
who slayed three thousand souls,
hanging their teeth in smiles around his thighs.
He was the plague, the drum, the axe;
the vampire darkly set upon the
striving speck of man.

He was the strange, red terror in the night,
the bogey of a child gone mad,
the blinding sun of blood.
He rode the fiendish nightmare
with a cry of baleful glee,
letting loose the scream of the tortured
on the rack of life.

And, finally, he was death
that closed the opened book.

Ω

© By Peter Mardon 1972.

# The Colour of Man

The air was laden
with the smell of summer.

Birdsong,
like gems glinting in the golden glow,
hung in the air.

Shadows etched beneath the many shades
and shapes of trees;

flowers bloomed profusely
making overglad the bees.

A tiny glimpse of Eden,
no hint of war or tension,
only peace and joy.

Here
every man was brother,
for in this summer glow
they were all
one colour–
that of Man.

© By Peter Mardon 1972.

# The Captive

My mind awoke to find itself within
a web of witchcraft, devilry and sin.
No light there was, that came from friendly day,
but only gleams of evil lit my way.

However I had been transposed to here
I did no know; I only knew the fear
of horrors foul unknown; and then the shock
of hearing some-one bolt an unseen lock.

Somewhere was freedom and the light of day,
but here within this horror did I lay.
Why was I here? And who had done this deed
My mind upon the answers tried to feed.

But reason for this prison knew I not,
nor who it was that made this place my lot.
I rose, and gazed around–the walls were stone,
and seemed to give a green light of their own.

Some quality they had, that made them strangely glow,
but why and how, my reason did not know.
A corridor it was, that turned and turned,
but not a door or window, soon I learned.

An endless passage made of dank, green stone
became my lot; and here I walked alone.
Sometimes the light was brighter than before;
sometimes 'twas darker–Thus is seemed, the core

-1-

of brightness came from out the clammy wall.
Apart from that, there was no light at all.
I walked and walked, a thousand miles it seemed
And often wondered, if perhaps I dreamed.

But 'twas no dream, but stark reality,
and never, did it seem, would I be free.
A maze of weird tunnels met my view;
some turning right, some left, some false, some true.

And ever did the green light come and go,
and wide, then narrow was the passage. So
I scarcely knew if I had doubled back,
or if perhaps I walked the selfsame track.

My mind was reeling for I felt that I
within a giant whirlpool, mad, did lie.
I tried to call aloud. Perhaps some other fool
Was also walking here–the madman's tool.

But only hollow echo made reply.
I wondered then if I was left to die.
But who would wish me dead? There were some men
who would go to lengths so cruel. The Prince of Enn

was one well noted for his evil streak!
But I had rescued him–would he then wreak
so foul and end for one who was his friend?
The answer, in confusion, found no end.

-2-

The hours passed, and hunger took its toll,
I scarcely could control my famished soul.
Then suddenly, like lightning, there he stood–
Young Peter–in his hand the needed food.

I rushed to him, and clasped him in my need,
and cried, "Now you are here, we surely shall be freed."
His smile was strange, he gave the food to me;
I ate it all, then cried, "Now we'll be free!"

But even as I spoke, the stupor came,
I scarcely even heard him say my name.
Thus as I fell into the stupored sleep,
I heard young Peter say, "Now shall I keep

you here forever, Michael. Yes, 'tis I
who have you prisoner. But, for now, goodbye."

© By Peter Mardon 1972.

-3-

# The Boy

The boy ran through the ocean's door,
a silver leaf clutched in his hand.

Within his eyes was knowledge
tinged with truth,
but he could not remember his name.

Only a few more steps remained
to tell the time;

but the pendulum swung
and struck him on the brow.

The boy fell down
as a leaf in Autumn
and did not stir again

until the clock
had reached the hour of three.

Then Destiny caught him up again
in eager arms
and flung him to the wind.

© By Peter Mardon 13.1.1972.

# Borderland

The silence of the night
does not worry us
with its
restful labour

in its shadows
images are
                  lost
new one can
                  begin.

The quiet of
our souls
                  is
                  never known
until
        we meet
        upon
        the borderland
of
    dreams.

© By Peter Mardon 1972.

# Bones

The bones blanched white
and
mocked the crimson sky
outliving
              thought and flesh;

   something           in the way
                         they spoke
eclipsed the sun
made foolish
the dreams
          of man.

The man of dreams
stands
       briefly
upon time's
          hot sands;
till death
          wears
          his bones.

© By Peter Mardon.

# The Beggar

He wore the years of his life
like and old tattered coat
that sheltered him
from cold and hurt
and prying eyes,
revealing little of what
lay beneath.

That was a world
that only he could know;

for here,
he alone was king.

No matter how cold
and rough and desolate
that land could be,
it was his own;
his only real possession,

except for the old tattered coat.

© By Peter Mardon 26/1/72.

# Haiku's

1.
The memories of
plants lie sleeping in the earth;
waiting Spring's next call.


2.
The sky
Is wrinkled
With nimbus clouds, like a babe's
face about to cry.

© By Peter Mardon 26/1/72.

# Hyacinth No. 2

Hyacinth,
you saw the child of clay,
the out-of-focus eyes
that prised within
the cave
of time's decay.

The rocks,
the stones,
the rotting, half-dressed bones,
tried to spell
for him
his past,
his future;

failed and turned to hell
his silent day;
until

your green,
your crown of blue
drew
those searching eyes to focus,
drew and held
to vision strange and new.

Time wore away
his robe of clay,
and freed
the fragile reed;

while you,
too,
shed your time,
your spring,
and both, together
found
another clime.

© By Peter Mardon 16th February, 1972.

# Haiku

See how the lizard
darts rom rock to rock, as if
he is made of fire!

© By Peter Mardon 1st Feb. 1972.

# Haiku

On the horizon,
trees nestle into the sky,
like buds on a bush.

© By Peter Mardon 1st Feb. 1972.

# Haiku

At sunset, crickets
sing the story of the day
in a higher key.

© By Peter Mardon 1972.

# Love Song

I sit in the dusk of evening
watching shadows lengthen
knowing that
when i am with you
it is
      forever sunlight.

Come with me
into the curve of night
let me kiss
the unspoken question
upon your lips
you will find
      the answer
sweeter than honey.

Let us watch the stars
eternal flight
      and with our
      love
weave new patterns
in the air
that future lovers
may behold as
      flights of stars.

The whisper of the morning
blends with your sigh
as we stir
beside each other
with the new-born earth
to greet the dawn.

-1-

Sunlight spins a golden crown
upon your hair
My eyes are amazed anew
and their love
permeates to
the depths of my soul.

All time has become
one for us
          for we are one
and Love is the
golden flowers
set upon Evening's brow
It is the star
that lights our
          night
that wakens our
          dawn
sustains the noonday sun
for Love has
          made us
                  one.

© By Peter Mardon 8th February, 1973.

# Re-Union

Driftwood of our broken time
left fragmented
                and distant
cast again into the vortex
of our hope
                and seen again
through open portholes
of desire

                With you i could
skip the patterns of
the world
                stringing universes
of forgotten dreams
across the windows
of our soul.

                Lover
take my hand
reach again
                into the
yearnings of eternity

There
        you will find
                me
waiting as ever
to
        clasp you
            in
                my love

© By Peter Mardon 9th February, 1973.

# The Other Road

I stood before the Crossroads. One was gold;
The other road was lonely, rough and cold.
The golden road led straight to Paradise,
The other road could claim the soul as price.
I saw the multitude go running past;
Their eager feet toward the Gold were cast,
For Rumour had it that and Angel fair
Was waiting in His glory for them there.
Though none had seen the Angel, yet they knew
That what they had been told must be true.

There came from out of Nowhere, Stranger dark,
Upon his brow he bore the cursed mark;
The mark that warned no man to be his friend,
Else would he also share the other's end.
His face was etched with misery and woe,
The cause of his exile he did not know,
But ever must he walk the lonely road
And bear the awful guilt, the heavy load,
Not knowing whence, or where, or even why,
But, scorched with anguish, left alone to die.

And even then, 'twas Hell would be his lot,
His bed would be foul Hades' furnace hot.
Yet did he bear his grief with noble pride,
But from the world his torment could not hide.
'Twas down this Other Road I saw him turn,
The lonely road from which is no return;
Where only desolation, woe and pain
Can share the journey and torment the brain.
The lonely, silent figure dared to take
The Other Road, and I began to shake.

-1-

What did it matter if he was outcast?
My struggles and my victory were passed,
By Heaven's highest God had I been blessed,
And told to take the Golden Road to rest.
But as I stood before the Crossroads there,
I felt within my heart, his own despair.
With arms outstretched to clasp him, did I run,
I did not stop to wonder what I'd done,
I only knew I could not turn away,
I could not take the Gold, and leave the Clay.

The warning voice from Heaven in my ear
Could not persuade my change. Not even fear
Of Hades' horrid furnace made me pause;
It did not matter if they shut the doors
And barred me out of Heaven; I would stay
Beside the exiled Stranger, share his way.
If 'twas to fiery torment, still I'd go
To share his lonely exile, ease his woe;
For what could heaven offer me,
If loss of him I loved was penalty?

Then, as the Judgement sounded through the All,
I saw the cloak from off his shoulders fall;
He turned, and he was Angel in disguise,
He had not waited in His Paradise,
But He had walked among us just to see
If He was cursed and exiled, who would be
The one to share His lot, and His exile,
'Twas I who won the Everlasting Smile.
But deep within my heart, I did not care
Where e'er we went, as long as He was there.

© By Peter Mardon 1973.

# Three Pet Cats

My three companions
sit nestle lie

images of black
grey
black and white

they know my mood
I theirs
we share the days
knit the hours
with our love

the sky may change
the light may dim
our mood does not

we share
peace

the light in
their eyes
green gold bright
does not dim

it says
we care to be
here

I care, too.

© By Peter Mardon 25/9/74.

# The Wanderer

He always walks alone.
The solitary sea-shore,
smooth, round pebbles and
the sunshine are his home.

His pace is always slow.
Why hurry? World will wait;
Evolution took a
billion years to grow.

His food is always humble.
Nature's bounty, riches
of the Universe are
his to mix and crumble.

Some say he's lived since first
the world began; he learned
the secret from the One
who let the bubble burst.

His eyes are calm and shine
with inner light. Some say
one day he'll wear a robe
and win a crown divine.

© By Peter Mardon 1974.

# Depression

deep-sea depths have dragged me in
no more swimming
just drowning in the love-worn water of tomorrow's
oblivion
seas of fish pass over
nudge
remind
the world still floats while I
sink drowning
lost in the flood of words
the pen shackles my wrist
drags me down
yet up
reaching sinking yet somehow
like the rest
still floating like scum
on the mirror
that reflects
not me but
who I am.

i am a muddy pool, a storm, and ocean full of words
there is no turning round no turning back
the wind howls and bangs at my open ears
the storm's store of stories
haunts my mind
to be free
unfettered
like i used to be
to feel the arms of love
encircling all i am like a gold lassoo
i weep i wait i wonder
cannot know
return my soul to its happy hunting ground
where there is you and me and me and you
forever in a circle up and down
round and round
my head is a top
it will not stop
untie me i cry
but only the will of god of who binds me round
what am i anyway?

© By Peter Mardon 11/2/75.

# Help Me

treacherous tides are in my mouth
they overflow
forgive me god
i do not know
assist one who loves too much
who treads a sea-worn path
where shells are rough and broken teeth
cut every wound
froth of the foam spits up
i am consumed
sweeps and swirls the crackling wave
each head a centaur
each eye a spear
aquarius they say this is
golden time to come
my time is black
sea-dark
and ocean green
tides are whips that lash me to the shore
crush my bones with shells that weep
and gash and grind and claw
somebody help me
help me
i am down
crowns of storm and lightning scorch my brain
i can't go down again

i must go up
where he has made his home
where grass is sweet and green
and skies are blue
but most of all where he is young and strong and true
pebbles slip beneath my feet
gold is a heavy load
the pen scratches and pricks
overthrown the heart of joy and peace
forgive me lord
i am weak and full of love
can it be taken up
can time be changed?
my heart is turned to lead and cannot move
wind rustles the pages of my mind
shifts the theme
no dream is
worth the loss the wait of love
my love for man is not as great as my love for one
let them all wait
i cannot

© By Peter Mardon 11/2/75.

# Bridge of Memories

Beneath the Bridge of Memories
we huddle
sifting grains of gold
amid the sand,

and telling tales
that reach
beyond the mean hut
of Existence.

© By Peter Mardon 1975.

# Roots

I have always listened
to the song
of the trees.

They wind their arms
around my dreams
and in the rustle
of their leaves
I hear
the patter
of my running feet.

So …
I measured pace with the trees
and found
that I too
had roots.

© By Peter Mardon 1975.

# Longing to Begin

I would alter the beat of my drum,
I would turn the tide of my sea,
If into my barren world you'd come
To share my life with me.

Together we'd soar in the azure sky
Two eagles with one heart-beat;
As over the mountains and plains we'd fly,
Longings and dreams complete.

But I am the river, and you are the wind,
I tremble and thrill as you pass.
And when you have gone, my sun has dimmed,
My stars are grown pale and sparse.

So pause for one moment, beloved, I pray,
Let our heartbeats entwine as one;
Let us share for a moment this golden day,
And my life will have begun.

© By Peter Mardon 29/8/76.

# Cross-Country-Witches

wishes like
   wizened witches
      hover around me
         as i sit hungrily
            eating my thoughts
               there is a
               pathway it
               leads to desire
            or someway to
         destruction
not until the
   final footprint
      marks the page
         with the mad frenzy
            shall I know
               whether to
                  sweet desire
                  or swift
                     destruction

© By Peter Mardon July 71.

# Syllabic Verse

A dear child, drowning:
a seedling, strong in Autumn,
deluged by Winter.

The world spins around
with as much rhyme and reason
as a maddened head.

This morning, the dew
was like teardrops hanging from
smiling angels' eyes.

Memory: a room
full of junk where lies hidden
a few precious gems.

See how the sun smiles!
it is almost as though the
buttercups were out.

Joy is like a gift
of daffodils, tied with gold,
on a sunny day.

Sorrow is like rain
falling at night on a house
that has no garden.

Love is like a house
once empty, suddenly filled
with golden flowers.

-1-

They are drawn to her
like blowflies that eagerly
pollute rotten flesh.

Solitude is like
an apple-tree that bears but
one golden apple.

A lover's embrace:
a tiny seed, nurtured in
the heart of the earth.

A lover's farewell:
crystal raindrops, reflecting
a empty mirror.

The snow lay like a
chaste maiden in her arctic
sanctuary … dead.

for a diversion
let us walk backward to see
what we left behind

in the East the Sun
rises, attempting to catch
himself in the West.

Thinking on the past
we fail to see what meets us
with the present's gift.

-2-

Her fast-falling tears
brought forth a river so wide
that he could not cross.

Solitary man,
defying the river's flow!
How brave … but foolish.

Sunlit lawns are green;
Moonlit lawns are more than green
Lovelit lawns are clouds.

You are more lovely
Than any flower that grows–
though you have no teeth.

© By Peter Mardon (27/9/71).

# Co-incidence?

A tear
that dropped from her eyes
was soaked up
    by the warmth
    of the sun;

became a crystal droplet
in a cloud,
  fell
  and caused to germinate
  a seed;

 the shoot that grew
became a floral plant;

 it bore a bloom;
they placed it
    on her grave.

© By Peter Mardon 10th October 1971.

# Backward–To Normality

I woke up this morning
to find that my soul
had become a blazing,
crimson thing.
                Rather perturbed,
                I gathered myself
                into the oldest,
                blackest coat I
                could find in my
                scant wardrobe,
and proceeded
to walk backward;
        hoping
        in this way
      to avoid my darling
      friends, who are always
      so intent on rushing
      forward.

It was not until
            the sun had
            finally set
            that
                  I reached
my destination.

As the sun's blazing light
   descended below the horizon,
     so did my soul
       lose its flaming
                 glory.

I breathed a sigh of
                 pale relief;
          and joined
       my pallid
     friends
for the nightly game
of chance
     and make-believe.

© By Peter Mardon 20th October, 1971.

# Mad Gloria

     gloria sits quietly combing her
long, golden hair. pauses, pregnant
with open questions, melt drunkenly
within her cream-smooth hands.

     strange songs mystic forth from
the tearing teeth of gloria's
magic comb. comb, comb …

     gloria's teeth are white and
gleam like a strand of beautiful
sea-washed pearls. gloria smiles,
comb smiles, and pearls clatter
and run down over the rocks, like
meteors freed from a frenzied
sky.

     sea reclaims its own gift … and
comb washes out on lilting waves
of song.

© By Peter Mardon 1972.

# Reflect

Spring cannot promise more
than Winter gives; empty arms
are generous arms.

Autumn fades away the
gifts of Summer, and patiently
we await.

Where-ever I go, there
is always more to be found
in the empty huts than in
the full ones.

© By Peter Mardon 1972.

# The Joke

the joke that leapt
up at me from
the printed page

and laughed at
me because I
tried to find

some hidden depth
of meaning, some
veiled, symbolic

cause or reason
to justify myself
and it; then

both sick, we
gave up

© By Peter Mardon 1972.

# The Wayward Wife

Between the parted pages of your eyes
the storm of wander brews.

I try to block the door but the wind
of your want is greater than my need.

My pain bleeds blood-red roses, spewing
them across your patterned path

in hope that you might, for even
three silken seconds, pause

to gather them to their sisters, who
flame crimson in your breast.

But the storm has flung its debris, and
the darting arrows of your glance

miss those fallen roses, oft-times seen,
for the rarer, rotten cast-offs

of the storm. One boom of thunder
as the door cracks shut, and I am left

alone, with only rotten leaves, the
tortured, broken branches of a tree,

once tall and straight, sad creaking of
some dying roots, and three fallen roses.

© By Peter Mardon 1972.

# Quandry

swamplands of soul are soft … grey
… squelchy;
      echoing,
          like lonely gulls,
      the melancholy call
      of
promise unfulfilled.

    view ahead
imbued with
        tantalising Magic,
          calling
    through golden trumpets
'step forth
        and
            claim your inheritance.'

miseries of the past
      are
          left behind
    but
        will not rest;
in tattered shrouds
            rise
    from open tombs.
            wailing,
'come back;
      soothe our weeping wounds,
      lull us
        into
          soft, sweet sleep
        of
          oblivion.

-1-

uncertainty freezes thought and limb;
go back
   regain, remould;
 or
   forward leap
    unlock
    the
      golden cask
      of
        tomorrow.

the fickleness of time
flickers its
     zig-zag loom
     and
  the moth
    flutters
   to
     the fiery flame
  oblivious
     of
      content
      and
       reward.

© By Peter Mardon 1972.

# Peace By The Pool

Two boys sat beside the pool,
the elder wearing the
peace sign
on the front of
his blue T-shirt.

In his hands glowed
a bright yellow scoop.

Water-lilies flashed their
colours up toward
the golden sun;
frogs croaked
sun shone, causing
shadows to cool the grass
beneath trees.

The boy in the blue
T-shirt,
scooped and scooped
again,
into the water of the pool,
and nearly overbalanced.

Peace was everywhere
on this warm and shaded
summer day;
everywhere, except in
the lilied-pool
where tadpoles swam
joyous in the freedom of life,
longing
one day
to croak as their parent-frogs
croaked …

but
"scoop!" went the peace-boy,
and half-a-dozen taddies
lost their freedom
and their
peace.

© By Peter Mardon 5/1/72.

# Cycle

The man in the khaki overalls
circled the tree;
and ocean of green
sprayed out
behind his buzzing machine.

The grass,
crowned with its many-flowered
heads,
shuddered to see him come;
yet
even more green
it grew
from its cut-off life.

So must the pruning of life
take place
allowing
the future green
and further flowers
their place,
that they, too,
might see the selfsame sun
and comprehend the
cycle of life-death-life.

© By Peter Mardon 5th January, 1972.

# Sea-Gulls

The water
like a fine white mist
blew across the lawn,
aided in its gossamer flight
by the gentle summer breeze.

The sea-gulls revelled
in the downy spray
spreading their wings
and pecking at the
newly-mown grass.

Two began to fight
over one worm.
The harmony became disjointed;
then,
in perfect unison,
they rose
and flew away …

The gardener had come
and turned
the water off.

© By Peter Mardon 5th January, 1972.

# The City-Girl

The city-girl came
to reclaim
her lost health
amid our sprawling hills
and deep, mysterious
green valleys.

Growing up in this
non-city-wilderness of
trees and birds and creek,
I learned to dread
the black bull
that bellowed through my
eleven years of wonder.

I tried to cast out
this dark bull-fear
by leaving the city-girl
to face the foe alone,
while I
stood safe,
outside the paddock-fence.

© By Peter Mardon 10th January, 1972.

# The Bull
## (Childhood Recollections)

I remember him–
the great, black bull
who roared through
the canyons of my mind,

when,
running bare-foot
and naked through
the streets of
our village

I was caught, savagely,
by the black curls at
the nape of my neck,
and

flung to kiss the
burning soil, whose
lips had pressed his hooves.

© By Peter Mardon 18th January, 1972.

# The Story-Teller
## (Childhood Recollections)

At eighty-four
great-grandfather still wore
thick grey curls,
                    watched
the world through
piercing eyes,
              his back
as straight and strong
as at twenty-one.

        At twenty-one
he wooed
his pretty ladies,
                    weaving
tales of brave-adventure
do-or-die;
              some true,
most make-believe.

        At eighty-four
he sat me on his knee,
                    droned
my seven years to sleep
                        with
tales of brave-adventure
do-or-die;
              some make-believe,
most true.

© By Peter Mardon 18th January, 1972.

# Hagar's Homecoming

The hour of the witch
fell upon
         the shadowed forest,
like a hawk
         descending upon
         an innocent prey.
Hagar was
   coming home,
              and
bats, toads, frogs
and mice
         told the tale.

Witches, high and low,
           trembled,
like slender saplings
caught within
         a tempest,
for the stealer
of spells
         was come among them
         once again.

Overhead
         the moon withdrew,
enveloping
the terror-striken
              in
darkness born of fear.

-1-

           Only one little
    lizard,
                  mindful of other matters,
                  dared disturb
                  the terror,
                        as he darted
    back and forth,
                  gathering,
                  storing,
    protecting knowledge,
    food for his
                  agile mind.

© By Peter Mardon 26/1/72.

# Little Boy Dead

When the little boy
died,
           the river ceased
           its flow;
the grass went into
mourning
              turning black.

Nature could not control
her sorrow,
              and wept rain
for seven days and
                nights.

The birds no longer
sang,
           and flowers hid
           their heads.
Such grief poured forth
it seemed
              the earth's
              great heart
would crack;
                then
on the eighth day,
the sun
           began to shine,
           birds began
                  to sing,
the flowers smiled again,
and
    the river
              overflowed.

© By Peter Mardon 27/1/72.

# The Listening Shells

Along the beach
the sea-shells heard the
        story of the waves,
vibrating
        to varying sounds
        made musical
                by
        repetition.

        The sand, in turn,
told the waves
        that
gentle Hesta's feet had
caressed their hearts
            that morn,
with pitter-patter song
of
    youthful love;

        carrying
in her soft-dove hands
the
        still-beating heart
        of
            her lover,
            whose corpse
now lay,
warm in blood,
            telling
            its own tale
to the
        ever-listening shells.

© By Peter Mardon 27/1/72.

# Haiku

Grass kisses the feet
of those who tread gently, and
frowns upon the rest.

© By Peter Mardon 1st Feb. 1972.

# Useless Spring

What value has Spring,
with its sunshine and flowers,
if you are not here?

© By Peter Mardon 28/1/72.

# Eclipse

The moon wears a blush,
as earth intercedes with the
sun, to cast a shade.

© By Peter Mardon 1st Feb. 1972.

# Haiku

The flowers open
their hearts to the sun, because
he smiles upon them.

© By Peter Mardon 1st Feb. 1972.

# The Robin Sings

The robin sings;
he does not see
the finger
poised to press
the button
tagged with death.

So does the child,
at birth
first cry,
then laugh
and sing;

unaware
that father's
loving-slaughter-hand
prepares
his bed of death.

© By Peter Mardon 16th February, 1972.

# Fabric

You who are my Springtime and my sun,
Come share with me the fabric of this day
We'll watch the wealth of Beauty spun
Into an iridescent Spring bouquet.

© By Peter Mardon 7/9/76.

# Await

I am a barren tree
a tree in Winter
when all the leaves are gone
and stark brown branches
reach mutely to the sky

The sap is gone from me
My bones are dry

Silent, I await the Spring,
the quick renewal,
the green flush of leaves
and blush of blossoms

Then will I sing,
a new song
the one imprisoned in my heart
this whole Winter long

Be patient, Love, await,
the barren tree is bursting at its seams
with heady wine of Spring
And all to thee will it bring.

© By Peter Mardon 8/9/76.

# A Lover's Lament

My love, I sit in silent solitude
Bowed down, alas! with deathly lassitude
And only you, my love, can change my mood.

Before we met, I lived a life serene,
Where skies were always blue and grass was green.
I did not know the shades that go between

But then our love burst into golden flower,
We lived and laughed and filled each golden hour.
How could I know the cream of life would sour?

So now you're gone and I am all alone,
I cannot weep, I cannot even moan
And in the mist of sorrow I am thrown.
Come back, my love! And make my life your own.

© By Peter Mardon 8/9/76.

# Love of My Heart

Love of my heart, can I be sad
When there's so much to make me glad?

Your own dear presence is, to me,
the greatest gift eternally.

And if that were not enough,
You shower me with your sweet love.

The beauty of the Spring is here
With bird-song singing true and clear.

About us blossoms every tree,
The grass is green as green can be.

Golden are the daffodils,
And all the air with perfume fills.

Such beauty does this season bring
That in its web I can but sing.

Love of my heart, can I be sad
When there's so much to make me glad?

© By Peter Mardon 13/9/76.

# A Poet's Prayer

Teach me, O Lord, the way to live
Upon his planet Earth
Teach me to love my fellow-man,
To understand his worth.

Give me, I pray, a humble heart,
Yet pride to live life well,
So that I may, with rich or poor,
In like condition dwell.

Bend me, dear Lord, that I may yield
A harvest so divine,
That others may follow the way I go,
Finally to be thine.

© By Peter Mardon 8/9/76.

# Sorrow's Gift

When I told you
that I was leaving
your tears
like raindrops fell
into the well of my heart.

and
a tiny seed
lying dormant there
burst into life

and
produced a flower
the like of which
I have never seen before.

© By Peter Mardon 1977.

# Blindness

The tenderness
with which
you won my love
blinded my eyes.

The ruthlessness
with which
you cast me aside
blinded my eyes

with tears.

© By Peter Mardon 1977.

# Gratitude

You said
you would meet me
beside the jasmine vine

When you did not come
I cried

And the jasmine
thanked me
for the rain.

© By Peter Mardon 1977.

# The man without a coat

The night overflowed with loneliness
and pain, as the man without a coat
began his usual battle against the
cold and dark and hunger.

Inverted doorways were havens, anxiously
sought which became places for memories
to parade their kaleidoscopes; some gay,
some dull, and others dark as his own
unlit life

Minutes yawned into agonized hours
as the night rushed about his threadbare
soul taunting him with floating scarves
of laughter that drifted this way,

that way; caught up again by two lovers
sharing the honey-warm seclusion of an inverted doorway
near the man
without a coat.

© By Peter Mardon 1st February 1977.

# Dreams

The tattered dreams
        of yesterday
            flutter
            in fragments,
  catching occasionally
        upon the
cactii of today.
  Desperately
            they try
to attach themselves,
to hang on,
       before
                    the wind of change
        tears them loose,
to wander again
             homeless and unfullfilled;
    until
       other hands
       may reach
              with youthful zeal,
claim them
        for their own,
and
   perhaps
        mould them
        to structures
   proud and tall and white,
             that leap
        from this clay below
to kiss
       the feet of
            heaven.

© By Peter Mardon 28th September, 1971.

# The Sainted Witch

The river did not condem
the girl who walked
it's mirrored face

but those who saw it
happen called the priest
who called the girl a witch

A stake was carved
with sign to purify
her evil soul

but when the flames
began to roar the
river spat them out

The priest then named
the girl a saint and
every knee was bent

until she turned the
water into wine. They
stoned her then.

She turned the stones
to bread and asking
no reward fed the poor

This was too much:
they tore her limbs apart
and fed her to the dogs.

© By Peter Mardon 12/1/72.

# Night Magic

This old oil lamp
whispered many tales
as it flickered
across the room
to the sound
of madre's voice
and padre's
sad guitar.

Full of awe
I lay
silent and still,
wondering why
the day
had not
the magic
of the night.

© By Peter Mardon
(Childhood Recollections).

# Girl on a tram

Is she perhaps
a goddess
come to probe
this lower world?

Hair like golden
river flowing
freely down
her back;

eyes, a misty lilac
edged with blue:

gown of vivid colours
splashed with
symbols -
peace and love.

No:
there are too many
of her:

she could only be
a princess -
one of milliard daughters
of a King.

© By Peter Mardon 28/2/72.

# And I wonder

He stirs beside me and I wonder
what is it then that binds us
Limb to limb to walk this sap-worn
path from horizon to horizon.

Always searching distant trees to climb
and scan, weaning secrets from grass
grown soft beneath our heads deep
pressing as we leave our minds behind?

Is there a world outside ourselves,
or is it all merely a fantasy of illusion
sprung forth from questing minds and
hearts too full for love?

He stirs again, and I wonder, is it
limb to limb embrace of silent conversation
that offers now, upon the altar of the grass,
or shall we flash like sunlight, blinding, free?

© By Peter Mardon 31/1/72.

# Freedom

A black bird
 flew
  with a broken wing
 over dark, impenetrable depths
  fearful
   of being
    again imprisoned
 behind
  cold, dark bars
  that
  for so long
   had blocked
   his way
   to
    freedom.
 the night was dark
   so dark
  that the black bird
  melted
   into it's depths
and
 could not distinguish himself
from
 his surroundings;
    only
    the pain
    in his right wing
   told him that
    he was
    a thing apart.
 the darkness was
    interminable
  and
   the blackbird
   felt himself
  shrinking shrinking
  until
  he was
 only a tiny
   black spot
that
 disappeared
  within
   itself.

© By Peter Mardon 30th Sept. 1971.

# Hunger

Quietly sitting,
exhausted from
the battle of life,
I pondered,
"do we use time,
or does time use us?"

We think to make
full use of time,
by filling it to
the brim, until it
chokes, overflows;
and overwhelms us

But, in reality,
time is living on
us, eating away
our bones, brains,
nerves, sinews...

When we are gone,
time will have
eaten us.

We go;
time remains.

© By Peter Mardon 28th Oct. 1971.

# Happy-Mad-Good-Boy

I am mad, happily insane;
wearing my crown of craziness
like yellow ribbons
flying in the breeze.

Nothing worries me:
I can change a dragon
to a fly;
then swat him with my
crazy-easy-mind

The rain is falling diamonds:
I catch them in my hands
conceal them in my hide-away
in paranoia's lands.

I count the stars by number
and add them to my list;
I ride the roaring thunder
with the lightning on my wrist.

I am mad, happily insane;
There's no sorrow in my life.
I see only rainbows.
and flowers
and count the robins as my friends.

There are no wars in my world.
Everyone is smiling.
And Paradise is here and now;
not waiting in the future
for the good:

because everyone is good
in my world.

The blows of the children strike at me
as I shuffle crazily about.
are kisses from the angels:
I jig and skip and shout
in gratitude
for the blessings
showered upon me.

God (if there is a god)
must be good:
as the angels are good,
as the children are good,
as the world is good,
as I am good,
as I am mad,
happily insane
as they all must be:
just like me.

© By Peter Mardon 7th Oct. 1971.

# Real Love

When the stars of midnight turn upon their wheel
And o'er the plains of man, the patterns steal
That weave the night's dark mantle, he appears,
Who stands beyond the silence and the spheres.

His hand upraised, he waits to see who comes
To see who to his charm succumbs.
A thousand dreams wheel by, all too intent
Upon themselves, not one to him is bent.

But patiently he waits. The night is long.
The stars continue with their weird song.
While, far below, a poet sits and broods;
Kaleidoscope are his varied moods.

The waiter waits, his eyes intent on him
Awaiting till that pen grow dim
At last the poet casts his pencil down
His dark eyes wild beneath a frown

The word he seeks will not give up its name
The poet casts himself down, eyes aflame
Perhaps in sleep the word will free itself
And bring to him its meaning and its wealth.

The dark eyes close, the dream begins to weave
Within his mind. Then straightway did he leave
His form of clay and soar to heights above
The word he sought—that lead him—it was 'love'.
Up, up he soared, beyond the other dreams
The universe about him reels and streams
The one who waited extended out his hand
The poet caught it. Now he'd understand

That hidden thoughts and meanings have their place
Beyond the veil of learning and his face
As he awoke, the morning after, knew,
That love was real, was living, and was true.

© By Peter Mardon 29/8/76.

# "THE LAST MAN ON EARTH"

## A SHORT STORY

## BY

## PETER MARDON

© By Peter Mardon 9th August, 1980.

# "THE LAST MAN ON EARTH"

The old man's life was almost spent, but his eyes held a soft radiance as he grasped his son's arm urgently. His voice though at first inaudible gained strength as he spoke:

"The Great Plan is almost complete!" he said to the serious-faced young man beside him. "It is up to you now, Adam."

Adam tried to ease the old man against the blankets.

"Don't tire yourself with talking, father," he cautioned gently.

But the old's man's voice became even more urgent.

"No, Adam, do not stop me," he insisted, leaning forward again. "I must impress on you the importance of your future role here on Earth. It took mankind nearly three hundred years to phase the population down to the Twelve, of whom I am the last. We, in turn, were permitted to only have two offspring between us – you and your wife Eve, both of whom we had late in life. When I die, you will be the last man on Earth, with Eve as your mate."

He paused to gather his fast-fading strength. Then he went on: "It will be up to you to make sure that the extinction of the human race takes place as planned. Then, and only then, can the Earth return to her former beauty and peace."

"Don't worry, father," Adam assured the old man "I am fully aware of my responsibilities. Eve and I know we must never have any children. We certainly don't want to restart the cycle of pollution , violation and destruction that our ancestor perpetrated upon the Earth and her creatures. No, the Earth need have no fear of us. Besides," he added, his clean-cut, pleasant face relaxing into a smile as he looked at the girl beside him, "Eve is the only companion I want – except you, of course, father."

And Adam is my whole world," responded Eve, her beautiful violet eyes lucent with love as she looked at her tall, athletic husband, whose smiling hazel eyes and quiet charm had kindled her love into a steady flame. "We have no need of children to complete our happiness." she added.

"Good, good!" whispered Benjamin. Then his blue eyes ignited again. "There is one more thing." he said. "When you both grow too old and feeble to take proper care of yourselves, you must use these." He held out two small capsules. "When you take them you will fall into a seemingly natural sleep and die peacefully and painlessly."

Adam accepted the capsules.

"Thank you, father." he said. "I'll put them in a safe place."

A warm breeze, delicately perfumed by the beautiful garden surrounding the tent, stirred the old man's fine, silvery hair.

"Tell me,; his voice was wistful, "how does the Earth look now? My eyes have not seen too clearly there last few months."

It is almost the end of Spring," replied Adam, and the garden is full fragrance and beauty. You can almost sense the dark mystery of new roots beneath curling plants, the blossoms have nearly all turned to ripe luscious fruit, and the deep green majesty of foliage is fraught with swift glitter of butterflies' wings. The grass is tender green, the birds sing for joy, and everywhere the little creatures frolic with their young."

"Truly a beautiful Eden!" whispered the old man, his blue eyes misting with tears of gratitude. "Life has been very good to us, also, these last years. Our diet of grain, fruit and nuts has increased our health and our strength greatly. But now old age has caught up with me and I must leave you and our beloved Earth. Truly a beautiful Eden," he whispered again.

"But this time man shall not destroy the peace and beauty of Eden," promised his son fervently. "Eve and I shall tend it with loving care, and when we grow old and die, the Earth will be free forever from the blight of man."

Benjamin eased back against the blankets, his fine silvery hair making a halo about his handsome, aquiline face.

"I must rest now," he said. 'But before you leave me, Adam, would you bring me a sprig of blossom from my beloved orchard so that I may hold it and breathe in its perfume?"

Adam left the tent and in a while returned with a sprig of pale pink blossom.

"Almost the last sprig left." he smiled. "The fruit is already ripe on some of the trees."

He placed it in his father's hands, noting how well they complimented each other – the delicate, snowy-pink blossom and the strong but gentle hands.

"The Earth rewards us generously for her release," said Ben. He held the blossom against his face. "How deliciously soft and fragrant it is!" he murmured. "Truly the plan was a wise one. I shall rest now." He lay back, his face beautiful in its serenity.

"Sweet rest, father Ben," whispered Eve. She kissed him on the forehead, then followed Adam from the tent.

That evening, as the filaments of a radiant sunset were weaving their prodigal way through the lacy patterns of the garden, Ben died.

Adam wept for the old man whose gentle but stimulating company had made him more than a father.

"You mustn't grieve for him," said Eve gently. "He was happy and content. He knew the Great Plan was almost complete."

+

They laid Ben to rest in the orchard he so dearly loved. As they returned to the tent, the sun, a huge, glowing red ball, began to sink below the distant hills, while the cool and sable wind caressed their skin with its long, delicately perfumed fingers. Then, as the wind subsided, and the garden lay hushed and still, they could almost feel the soft impact of the shadows as they fell.

Adam put an arm about Eve's slender shoulders. She smiled up at him.

"We have each other," she said. " And a beautiful world in which to live."

That night, the sky was a deep, antique blue with stars shimmering in the distance.

As held his wife in arms, he thanked Providence for such a beautiful and loving mate. She was surely the most beautiful woman ever to have lived on Earth; her skin so smooth and the alabaster clear against long, lustrous chestnut-brown hair, while her dark-fringed violet eyes shone continually with love. Even her mind was full of tender thoughts that constantly blossomed into loving ways.

It wasn't until Dawn was casting soft ribbons of pink and gold over the far hills that they finally drifted off to sleep.

One of the others re-entered the space-ship, and in a matter of moments, the sky was alive with ten thousand space-ships that had been hovering out of sight awaiting their leader's command.

Like a swarm of silver locusts they descended toward the defenceless Earth.

Adam tried to rise, to protest, but fell forward on his face. He was dead.

So was the Great Plan.

# Phoenix

The wheels of time
like
      dying birds
           grew still,
sending the stars
like figs,
      across the sky.
         The boy
sat still,
      eyes wide
      but calm and proud
his kingdom had
         departed;
but the tiny, silver key
would endure
and
      open wide the door
of hope
      and
peace.
      The universe subsided
    and was still.
         Then,
from the ashes
rose
    the phoenix.
         Together
the boy and phoenix fled
to some far-distant
        call,
where grew
      no seeds of time;
and both
      forgot
the former taste and
         tread.

© By Peter Mardon 14th January, 1972.

# About the Author

He was a spirit entity know as Peter Mardon; who was a walk-in, using the vehicle of the late Fler Beaumont (a medium). A walk-in can mean; the original soul of a living body departs and a different spiritual entity enters. How long it wants to remain and what its motive is, needs to be addressed; before permission is granted from the owner of the body, for this unusual event to happen. His poems reveal a magnificent body of work during the 1960s and 1970s.

His poems are a tour-de-force from an incredible young male spirit.

They are confronting and disturbing in areas and raise issues of the human spirit, and it's mortal experiences.

They are also very lyrical, with moving messages that resonate with the works of R. Tagore and K. Gibran.

There are seriously powerful poems of the forces of darkness and light, and divine cosmic poems encompassing eternal love between higher entities.

His short story written in 1980 was well before our current climate awareness.

His animal protection activism also was much valued by those in the field and his ideas gained root in other charity areas and spread a vital message; of human & animal interconnection. He knew both areas are on this life journey, to love & support each other, & our beautiful environment.

His poems reflect images & insight that could see into other minds & other levels of being; even spotlighting past lives & its experiences.

When he finished his meaningful journey though not in the body all the time, & left the medium (Fler) after 7 years, the friends he had made, in that time, were bereft. We reassured them, they would meet him again, as his being was truly alive, in another dimension, which could be accessed after passing to higher life.

## "Greater Far"

*Published in "Phoenix Australia"- December, 1976.
Winner of Poetry Competition.*

The speck of dust looked up and saw the grass.
He said, 'O mighty one, I'll worship thee.'
The blade of grass just sighed and said, 'I pass.'
Then he looked up and saw the stately tree.

'O lordly one,' he cried, 'most surely you
Would be the greatest power that could be.'
The tree looked up to see the sky of blue,
And said, 'You are the one eternally.'

The sky, in humble worship, watched the star
That shone so brightly in the dusky night.
He said, 'O lovely one, you surely are
The one above the all, the power bright.'

The star gazed up, and said, 'I worship God,
For He's the one, the Holy One, most high.'
But God just smiled, and gave a knowing nod,
And said, 'I see a Greater Far than I.'

© By Peter Mardon 1968.

***

Comments by the Poetry judge, Mr Louis H. Clark: (author of Romance & Reality) in The Australian War Memorial. A WWII Poet, of renown.

'I have been associated with several poetry judges in the past but this is the first time I have experienced the sense of true poetic dedication and illumination.'

In "Greater Far" one is swept along and gathered up in this, "from microscopic to macroscopic unity" theme. The philosophy embodied in the poem would have been stupendous and audacious stated in plain, theological prose terms, but the poet's gift of presenting simple, telling imagery impresses the theory even more!

The title, probably spontaneous, with the use of 'Far' as a noun, embraces a 'becoming' in the conception of the Divine; "Greatest Far" would have suggested a finality, but "Greater" leads us to further outreach. The succinct summation in the last verse is splendid. The entire poem makes one agree with what Coleridge said of the poet, "he brings the whole soul of man into activity", and Emily Dickenson's comment, "he makes me feel as if the top of my head were taken off."

# 100% of profits of this book are going to Animals Australia. Available on Amazon 2022

*'To know even one life has breathed easier because you have lived. This is to have succeeded.'*

In Fler Beaumont, the animals have lost a cherished friend and advocate. Fler's path has forged a kinder future for those who share this world with us. Through the spirit of kindness and compassion, her legacy lives on.

Animals Australia
for a *kinder* world

# Sources and Acknowledgements

These are sincerely made, for the following individuals and publishers, for the use of certain itemised contents in this volume. If anyone has been accidentally overlooked, the next publishing will correct this oversight.

## Dedication Page

1. 'The Mystic Seer'-Spiritual Source
2. 'Extract from'-Alfred Baron Tennyson-1850. In Memoriam-A.H.H. (Publisher-E. Moxon-London). 1850.

## Front Cover & Back Cover Images

1. Front: Coloured Star Plate-By Kind Permission of Keith P. Cooper-Pole Star Publication LTD. U.K. 2006. (Astronomy-The Grand Tour Of The Universe)
2. N.A.S.A.-Back Cover 'Mountains of Creation' JPL-Caltech/L. Allen/(Havard-Smithsonian cfa). (Astronomy - The Grand Tour of the Universe.)

## About The Author. P. 215

Grateful acknowledgemant to the LTE Mr. Louis H. Clark-Poetry Judge, comments in:
Phoenix Australia-December 1976.

He is a renowned W.W.II Poet. 'Author of 'Romance & Reality' now in The Australian War Memorial.

A special grateful acknowledgement to Paul Sandalis for his wonderful assistance with computer searches, e/mails, & unfailing support.

To Daniela DaPozzo for unfailing encouragement & Alex Salpietro for good suggestions and invaluable assistance.

Blaise van Hecke (in spirit) & Kev Howlett from Busybird Publishing. Grateful acknowledgement for their generosity & patience & assistance, I deeply valued, while compiling this book.

Grateful Acknowledgement also to:
Andrew McConville-State Library Victoria.

Lisa Gerber-Mannix Library.

Pamela Coutts-Author.

www.ingramcontent.com/pod-product-compliance
Lightning Source LLC
Chambersburg PA
CBHW070406120526
44590CB00014B/1274